Fuchsias

Fuchsias

A practical guide to cultivating fuchsias, with over 450 beautiful photographs and illustrations

JOHN NICHOLASS

PHOTOGRAPHY BY PETER ANDERSON

introduction

Above The large double flower of 'Irene Sinton', with its blush-pink sepals, a full lilac-blue corolla and splashes of pink on the petals. The opening flower bud, splashed with raindrops, is about to reveal its inner secrets.

This is a book for anyone who loves fuchsias. It describes how to grow them, which types are best for particular positions in the garden, and how to deal with any problems that might arise in their cultivation.

Fuchsias are superb summer flowering plants. They are fast growing, come in a range of flower colours and sizes and can be used in containers, hanging baskets and as summer bedding in the garden borders. These versatile plants also have a range of growth types – some are upright and bushy, others are trailing or cascading, and some, such as 'Lady Boothby', even have a climbing habit, ideal for decorating walls and fences. Fuchsias are very easy to train into different shapes, the standard fuchsia being well known.

The first section of the book gives a short history of this beautiful plant. Fuchsias grow in the wild mainly in the southern hemisphere, where their striking, exotic flowers flourish in the warm climate.

Next, a section on the fuchsia garden is packed with ideas for growing these rewarding plants, whether as temporary residents in a summer border or as permanent shrubs, even hedges. There are also tips for growing fuchsias in containers, using all sorts of exciting arrangements that will add splashes of colour to the garden throughout summer and autumn. And for those who really want to extend the growing season of these stunning plants, the book gives instructions for growing fuchsias inside the house, in the greenhouse or in a conservatory.

Then comes a section on practical gardening techniques, which explains how to select and buy fuchsia plants, how to train fuchsias into all sorts of shapes, take cuttings, keep the plants alive over the winter and deal with common pests and diseases.

The penultimate section is a comprehensive directory of over 200 fuchsia cultivars – from standards, trained structures and hanging baskets to hardies, Encliandras and unusual cultivars – with guidance about the ideal varieties for any situation. Finally, a calendar of care lists the appropriate tasks to be carried out in each season.

Every gardener, even those with a great knowledge of fuchsias, will be able to find something in this book to inspire them to try some different fuchsia cultivars or planting techniques.

Opposite A hardy fuchsia growing strongly against a high stone wall and partly covering an open wrought-iron gate.

Below Hardy fuchsias growing in a border, their dancing red and purple flowers contrasting with the green lawn. In the background there is a fruiting clematis vine with its delicate seed-heads scrambling over the fence.

THE FUCHSIA
garden

Fuchsias flower profusely in the summer, often blooming from late spring right through to the first autumn frosts. A greenhouse can extend that flowering period even further by allowing the keen gardener to raise plants in full flower that can be moved into the garden as soon as the weather allows. This chapter will give you many ideas for using fuchsias in a garden scheme. Hardy fuchsias make excellent specimen plants in the shrubbery, or can be used as an eye-catching dividing hedge. Large trained shapes make outstanding focal points to draw the eye. Tender fuchsias work well as summer bedding in groups or as individual plants, and smaller growing cultivars are ideal for edging in beds or in the rockery.

Left This splendid example of the hardy cultivar 'Margaret Brown', with its pretty single flowers, is more than 1.8m (6ft) tall, and looks attractive growing among other shrubs such as weigela and camellia.

Above 'Brenda White' is an attractive single-flowered cultivar which is perfect for a border edging plant or small standard. It has lightish foliage and a truly classic bell-shaped flower.

single specimen fuchsias

Large fuchsia plants look wonderful grown as specimen plants in large pots, planted in the ground in the main garden borders, or dominating a small border in a paved area. They can make a striking focal point grown against the right background – for example, you can choose a flower colour that contrasts well with a ground cover of chippings or slate.

Right 'Thalia', a Triphylla hybrid, has racemes of long brilliant red flowers contrasting perfectly with its dark olive-green leaves, and flourishes in full sun.

Below Large hardy fuchsias, dripping with red and purple flowers, growing over an attractive old stone wall. Many of these large hardy plants grow in milder areas, where they are not reduced to ground level by frosts each winter.

With such a range of flower colours and sizes, and a long summer flowering period, using fuchsias as specimen feature plants gives very satisfying results. If you are lucky enough to live in an area with mild winters, where the stems of hardy fuchsias survive, you can make them part of a permanent planting scheme. Otherwise, specimen plants need winter protection to survive. This will allow them to start into growth again in the late winter and early spring, and will ensure they look good each year. Large specimen plants can be formed from single plants trained as shrubs or bushes, or one of the trained shapes. Alternatively, to obtain a large specimen in a short time, the multi-plant technique works well.

Use these specimen plants to create a focal point on terraces or patios, in the middle of lawns, on the edges of wide steps, beside gates or

doorways or on large areas of gravel or stone chippings. They also look very striking in low stone or brick walls which have a planting area built into them, or in a square stone pot placed on top of a wide wall – as long as it is stable and cannot be knocked over or blown off by the wind. Pick the right fuchsia for the height of the wall – for a low wall, an upright-growing cultivar will look best, and for a medium or high wall a more lax cultivar will create a flowing, spreading effect.

SUNNY AND HOT AREAS

Triphylla hybrids are a natural choice for this sort of position, where they will reward you with continuous flowering through the summer. Grow them in the ground or in large porous clay pots to help keep the roots cool. This is one of the most important factors to ensure fuchsias do well when exposed to full sun.

Far left 'Richard John Carrington' is a bush cultivar and has medium-sized single flowers with bright cerise sepals and a blue-violet corolla. This compact hardy plant has light green foliage that ages to dark green.

Left *F. magellanica* var. *molinae* is a fantastic hardy fuchsia with vigorous growth, whose alternative US name, 'Maiden's Blush', comes from the small white and pale pinkish-lilac flowers.

Below 'Genii' is a superb hardy cultivar whose foliage becomes a vivid yellow-green in a sunny position, contrasting beautifully with the delicate red and purple single flowers. Here, it is growing by a path together with other shrubs.

DAPPLED SHADE AREAS

These are probably ideal areas to grow fuchsias, but they are not always easy to find in a small garden. Good examples are on the edges of the shade cast by open tree canopies, in the shade created by artificial structures, or near east- or west-facing walls. Most fuchsias will thrive in these areas as they recreate the conditions where the species grows naturally in the wild.

While you can use almost any of the fuchsia cultivars in these areas, the pastel-coloured varieties look at their best in dappled shade, as their flower colours intensify.

SHADY AREAS

Fuchsias will grow well in light shade, although this can reduce the amount of growth they will make in a season. An ideal situation would be a wall that gets the early morning and the late evening sun, painted white or a light colour, so that it will reflect any available light back on to the plant. Many of the white or light pastel-coloured fuchsias will do well here, as the whites stay really white in the shade.

Alternatively, you can use fuchsias with very dark flower colours that tend to be bleached by the sun; they will keep their colour in the shade, and will show up well against light backgrounds.

SINGLE SPECIMENS

Plants that form a good natural shape with distinctive flowers that stand out from the foliage are superb to use as specimen plants.

Full sun: 'Thalia', 'Coralle', 'Gartenmeister Bonstedt', 'City of Leicester', 'Falling Stars', 'Genii', 'Joan Pacey', 'Nancy Lou', 'Other Fellow', 'Tennessee Waltz'
Dappled shade: 'Border Queen', 'Lillian', 'Lady Kathleen Spence', 'Misty Blue', 'Rolla'
Shady: 'Alaska', 'Constellation', 'Evensong', 'Flirtation Waltz', 'Florence Mary Abbot', 'Iceberg', 'Lady Kathleen Spence', 'Ting a Ling'
Shady against white background: 'Gross aus dem Bodenthal', 'Haute Cuisine', 'Marin Glow', 'Ortenburger Festival', 'Roesse Blacky', 'Royal Velvet'

fuchsias as summer bedding

Many gardeners use a variety of plant types and sizes within summer bedding schemes and fuchsias can be very useful as part of these schemes. The best fuchsias for summer bedding are those that tolerate being in full sun and display their flowers well. There is quite a choice of available colours, both in flower and in foliage.

The summer garden border is the ideal spot for fuchsias of different growth sizes, leaf colour, and flower sizes and shapes. They will suit all sorts of bedding schemes, from mass planting to more informal arrangements. A useful tool in planning summer bedding schemes is the colour wheel, which gives a guide to complementary colours and can help the gardener to envisage the resulting mix of colours.

MASS PLANTING SCHEMES

Formal schemes for large areas require compact and uniform plants so that the edges in the design remain clearly defined, and several fuchsia cultivars fit these requirements. The raisings by Tabraham, including the 'Seven Dwarfs' series and the 'Thumbs', are ideal as they are very small and compact. Use them as edging plants in their own right, or interplant them with other suitable bedding subjects for edging. Alternatively you could plant them in blocks in a background of edging or ground-cover plants, which will contrast well against the fuchsia's foliage and flowers. The effect can look quite spectacular with the small fuchsia flowers moving in the breeze and sparkling in the sun, or lighter colours and whites standing out in the dusk. Avoid over-feeding these small cultivars to keep their dwarf and compact growth.

Fuchsias with variegated foliage are also worth using as formal summer bedding plants, since the leaf colours intensify in the bright light of the sun, and the growth becomes sturdier. Some cultivars worth trying are 'Autumnale', 'Sunray' and 'Tom West' (which is almost hardy). These have some of the best foliage colours, but they are not quite as compact, so are not suitable for edging.

Far left 'Tom Thumb', a compact hardy cultivar from France, introduced in 1850. It is seen here flourishing at the front of the border, contrasting with the perennial *Kalimeris incia* 'Charlotte'.

Left This Triphylla fuchsia in full flower makes a stunning sight against an *Aloe arborescens* in a hot terraced border with palm trees in the background.

PLANTS FOR MIXED BEDDING

Use fuchsias that grow to a fairly large size in mixed bedding schemes, either as single plants or in groups. The best cultivars are those that have upright and self-branching growth, display their flowers well and are happy in a sunny position. Some of the darker-coloured blooms bleach and fade with strong sunlight and many whites change to different shades of pink in full sun, so bear this in mind when choosing cultivars. The leaf colours of many fuchsias are mid-green, but some cultivars have quite pale or dark green leaves, so consider this when planning combinations. 'Lyes Unique' has waxy white sepals and a salmon-orange corolla and 'Jack Siverns' is a new, vigorous bush with aubergine flowers. The Triphyllas are excellent for summer bedding, for example 'Thalia' with its dark foliage and orange flowers, 'Coralle', with sage-green foliage and orange flowers, or how about trying 'Firecracker', the variegated leaf sport from 'Thalia'.

PLANTS FOR SINGLE PLANTING

Some fuchsia plants grow quickly into large spreading shrubs, and therefore they are excellent for planting as single specimens in the border or any other space that needs filling with summer colour. Some examples are 'Celia Smedley', 'Checkerboard', most of the larger *F. magellanica* variants and the larger Triphylla hybrids.

Left A meandering bed planted with a mixture of fuchsias with a pale foliage cultivar cleverly delineating the edge.

Above A fuchsia border, including 'Genii', 'Thalia' and 'Checkerboard', giving an impressive, flower-filled overall effect.

CULTIVARS FOR SUMMER BEDDING

The following are suggestions for fuchsias that are suitable for single-season use as a summer bedding plant for mass or single planting.

Edging or mass planting: 'Alwin', 'Bambini', 'Baroness van Dedem', 'Bashful', 'Ben Jammin', 'Doc', 'Dopey', 'Geoffrey Smith', 'Grumpy', 'Happy', 'Lady Thumb', 'Mischief', 'Sleepy', 'Sneezy', 'Son of Thumb', 'Tom Thumb', 'Tsjiep', 'Vobeglo'
Group or single planting: 'Bon Accord', 'Border Queen', 'Dawn Fantasia', 'Jack Siverns', 'Koralle', 'Nellie Nuttall', 'Nice 'n' Easy', 'Olive Smith', 'Pink Fantasia', 'Rose Fantasia', 'Rose Quartet', 'Snowcap', 'Thalia', 'Thamar', 'Tom West', 'Upward Look', 'Variegated Pink Fantasia', 'Walz Jubelteen'
Single planting: 'Alan Titchmarsh', 'Celia Smedley', *F. boliviana* and *F. boliviana alba*, 'Mrs Lovel Swisher', 'Other Fellow', 'Sharpitor'

standard fuchsias

One of the best ways to display fuchsias is by growing them as standards of different heights, making vibrant focal points around the garden. They look like small trees covered in flowers, growing at the ideal eye height, and from a distance attracting the eye to different parts of the garden, standing out against fences and hedges.

There are many places around the average garden that are ideal for placing standard fuchsias to enhance and improve the view. Some places to consider are either side of an entrance gate, next to a doorway, by a fence, against a non-flowering evergreen background such as a conifer hedge, in the hardy fuchsia border to change the height perspective, or in groups of several identical standards in a more formal border. Smaller standards look wonderful on the edges of steps, around patios or at the edge of ponds, and you can even use miniature standards in rockeries. Where the plant cannot be set in the ground, it will need some kind of support to keep the pot upright.

Above A half standard with pink and white flowers growing in an attractive pot. Standing on paving close to a gate, it makes a really eye-catching feature.

Right A standard of the hardy cultivar 'Lady Thumb' growing among ferns by a doorway, carefully placed to stand out against a white wall. The small flowers and compact bushy growth habit of 'Lady Thumb' make it an excellent plant for a smaller standard.

GATEWAYS, WALLS AND DOORS

One very striking place to put large standards is either side of a gateway, especially where the gate is built into a low boundary wall about 1–1.5m (3–4½ft) high. The wall will give a good anchoring point to support the standards and will afford them some protection, but they will still be easily visible to anyone using the gate. Another very good place for standards is as a feature either side of a front door, which creates a beautiful entrance to your home and makes a great conversation point for visitors.

CREATING EXTRA HEIGHT

Standards can be used to raise the height of other displays. For instance, in a group of pots of different sizes and heights, adding an appropriate-sized standard at the back of the group can create a much more impressive effect over the whole display. Use the same technique at the back of borders in front of hedges or fences, when some extra height is required, or there is a need for a focal point to draw the eye upward. Standards with white or lighter pastel-coloured flowers look splendid against dark fences and hedges, and deeper-coloured cultivars are better against light walls or golden-yellow hedges. Red and white flowers stand out well against mid-green hedges.

STEPS, PATHS AND BORDERS

Putting quarter standards at the edge of steps in the garden can create a very pleasing sight. They will help to both define the edges of the steps and soften the transition between the steps and the garden. Similarly, position them along the edges of paths, as long as the paths are wide enough, where they will help to delineate the borders. Quarter standards are also excellent planted in summer bedding borders, especially where many low-growing bedding plants are grown around them. This technique is often used in botanical gardens and other public displays.

Fuchsia standards also make excellent specimen plants, and placing a full standard in a small circular border in the centre of a lawn will make a very eye-catching sight. Plant the remainder of the circular bed with other bedding plants chosen to complement the height and colour of the fuchsia standard.

TERRACES AND PATIOS

Another exciting way to use standard fuchsias is along the edges of terraces or patios. If you are constructing a terrace or patio, a good tip is to sink some large pots into the ground around the edges to place the standards in during the summer. This technique will help to keep the roots cool and the standards upright. You can use these same pots for bulbs and spring-flowering plants, until the time comes to bring the standards out again in the summer. Half or full standards also look good set close to bench seats against light-coloured walls.

Right A full standard of the hardy cultivar 'Margaret' growing against an evergreen background, close to a bench seat and surrounded with colourful containers of ageratum, begonias and pelargoniums.

CULTIVARS FOR USE AS STANDARDS

The following cultivars are suggestions for growing different types of standards. The measurements show the length of the clear stem between the surface of the soil and the lowest branch of the head.

Miniature standard 13–25cm (5–10in): 'Baby Bright', 'Tom Thumb', 'Nellie Nuttall'
Quarter or table standard 25–46cm (10–18in): 'Genii', 'Katrina Thompsen', 'Chang', 'Paula Jane', 'Estelle Marie'
Half standard 46–76cm (18–30in): 'Olive Smith', 'Annabel', 'Checkerboard', 'Garden News'
Full standard 76–107cm (30–42in): 'Celia Smedley', 'Snowcap', 'Amy Lye', 'Achievement'
Weeping standard 46–107cm (18–42in): 'Eva Boerg', 'Jack Shahan', 'Falling Stars', 'Brutus'

aubergine fuchsias

Fuchsias with different shades of purple in the corolla have been in commerce for many years. As a further refinement of this colour, hybridizers started to release fuchsias in aubergine shades in the mid-1980s. The Dutch hybridizers,

especially Hermann de Graaff, introduced some beautiful and vivid aubergine cultivars, including 'Aubergine', 'Gerharda's Aubergine' and 'Haute Cuisine'. There is quite a choice of aubergine fuchsias with flowers of different sizes from small

'Black Country 21' This is a single-flowered cultivar with a tube and sepals of deep magenta and a violet to aubergine corolla. The erect blooms stand out on a compact and bushy plant with small mid-green leaves. It makes a nice small standard.

'Gerharda's Aubergine' This gorgeous trailing fuchsia has small to medium single flowers with a deep red/aubergine tube and sepals, and an aubergine corolla. It is excellent for growing in all types of baskets and hanging pots.

'Tarra Valley' This fuchsia resulted from an interspecies hybridization cross and has very unusual single flowers with a long light greenish-yellow tube, short greenish-white sepals and an unusually coloured dark red/aubergine/purple corolla.

'Haute Cuisine' A superb double-flowered cultivar with dark red sepals and a deep aubergine corolla, contrasting beautifully with its light to mid-green leaves. It has a stiff trailing habit and is excellent for baskets and containers.

'President George Bartlett' A semi-double cultivar with a burgundy-red tube and sepals and a deep aubergine corolla. It is excellent when trained as a standard, with its slightly lax growth habit. It was hybridized by Bielby/Oxtoby and released in 1997.

singles to large doubles, and habits of growth from trailing to strongly upright. New aubergine-coloured cultivars are still being released every year. The photographs on these pages give an idea of some of the cultivars that are available. An excellent way to grow them is as standards or in hanging baskets, so you can see the beauty of the flowers at eye level. They will also contrast well with pastel and white-flowered cultivars in mixed baskets, containers or planting arrangements. There are two aubergine fuchsias which are listed as hardy: 'Ben Jammin', a small compact-growing single, and 'Dorothy Handley', a vigorously upright semi-double that will grow 75cm (30in) in one season. A fuchsia that is good for summer bedding is 'President George Bartlett'. There are a number of lax types that can be used in baskets: 'Art Deco', 'Haute Cuisine' and 'Ratatouille' are examples of these. An attractive Triphylla type named 'Pabbe's Torreldöve' has aubergine-blue flowers.

'Ben Jammin' A small, compact plant, borderline hardy, superb for growing as a mini standard or a small pot plant. It has small to medium single flowers with aubergine sepals flushed pale pink and a dark aubergine corolla, and mid- to dark green foliage.

'Jack Siverns' This cultivar has a vigorous and bushy growth habit, and is excellent grown as a specimen plant or a standard. The flowers are single and medium in size with aubergine sepals blushed with pink and an aubergine corolla.

'Jessica Reynolds' A floriferous medium-sized single-flowered cultivar with beautiful aubergine sepals flushed white and an aubergine corolla. It has neat, compact self-branching growth and mid-green leaves.

trained fuchsias

A well-grown fuchsia trained into a shape like a pyramid or a fan can be a stunning sight and can make a real focal point in a garden. A large pyramid or pillar can make a striking free-standing display in the middle of a lawn, while a fan or an espalier can be trained to cover a large area of a wall or fence.

Right A magnificent fuchsia fan grown from the cultivar 'Lillian Annetts'. This structure measures more than 2m (6ft) high and wide and was grown by Chris Woolston.

Below *F. boliviana* is a fuchsia species from Bolivia, first described by Carrière in 1876. It is a vigorous, though tender, climbing shrub.

Before embarking on growing large trained fuchsias for display as specimens in the garden, it is important to consider how they will be stored for the winter, as they are best kept ticking over in green leaf. It is easier if you live in an area without frosts, where leaving them outside all year without winter protection is possible, but most growers will need at least a frost-free greenhouse big enough to overwinter these structures.

PILLARS AND PYRAMIDS

Large pillar or pyramid shapes will grow more than 3m (approx. 10ft) over a few years with the right care and growing conditions, but smaller specimens of 1m (3ft) or more in height may be grown in a single season and still make a very impressive show. As the plants age, the wood becomes harder and stronger and they are better able to stand the ravages of strong winds and heavy rains, but during the first year when green growth is maturing to wood, some extra protection and support is needed. It is therefore important to make sure the centre stake or cane is in good condition and strong enough, especially the part that stands in the compost (soil mix), which is more prone to rotting. The best time to change the cane is when you cut back the plant in the autumn. Use ties such as PVC tape, and check the tightness as the stem thickens. If the top of the cane is tied to an overhead support, that will minimize the chances of it being blown over.

Pillars and pyramids can be used in a similar way to large standards, but they look especially impressive when placed either side of a doorway, or at the edges of a patio or yard where they will help to highlight the corners and edges. They will also stand out beautifully as a feature in the centre of a lawn.

FANS AND ESPALIERS

The usual way to grow fans and espaliers is against a wall, where they can benefit from the shelter and warmth (especially if it is a house wall) and are easily supported. Choose a wall that receives a reasonable amount of sun, but not full sun all day.

Although espaliers are usually grown against a wall, you can also position them next to a wire fence, where they can be seen from both sides, as long as the fence is strong enough.

Large specimens of this type of structure, especially the fan shape, have large frontal surface areas. A specimen measuring 2m (6½ft) can present a surface area of 1–1½sq m (1.2–1.8sq yd). Therefore, it is important to secure it well against the wall, ideally by ties between the wall and the top of the framework, to prevent the wind from damaging it. When in full flower, this type of plant can be breathtaking, and is certain to be a focal point in your garden. It is well worth the effort required to move it to a warm place every winter, enabling it to grow to such an impressive size.

OTHER TRAINED SHAPES

Topiary shapes can be very successful if you place them in areas where they catch the eye, such as on low walls, perched on top of pillars by gateways, or even on purpose-designed stands. Ensure that you fix them securely so they cannot blow away and they are sure to create a lot of interest, whatever the shape. If you use the Encliandra types, allow them to flower, just clipping off any long growths to keep them tidy. Use small culture (miniaturized) versions of rings, fans and pyramids in similar ways.

CLIMBING FUCHSIAS

Some fuchsia cultivars have a vigorous, rampant habit of growth, which makes them very difficult to train in a conventional way. However, some of these make excellent climbing plants, grown permanently in a greenhouse, or against a fence, a pergola or a simple post, by using large plants started off in the greenhouse. Some fuchsias which are suitable for this are the species *F. boliviana*, *F. regia*, 'Lady Boothby', 'Royal Purple' and 'Wisteria'.

Right A vigorous hardy fuchsia looks quite at ease climbing naturally up a fence, covered in wild columbine and other creeping and trailing plants.

ESPALIER STRUCTURE

An espalier structure formed from a central stem and a series of strong horizontal laterals supported by a framework. The lateral side growths are tied in and carry the flowers.

blue fuchsias

Blue shades in fuchsia flowers vary from a lilac or lavender blue through deeper blues to violets in the corolla. White, pink or red sepals usually accompany them, and those with white sepals are ideal for shady corners of the garden.

Many fuchsias have names starting with 'blue' but some of these have no blues at all in the flower, so do look carefully at the description in a catalogue. There is still no real royal blue fuchsia, but plenty of pale blue fuchsias of a similar shade to

'Delta's Sara' This is an upright vigorous cultivar with beautiful semi-double flowers with white sepals and a mid- to deep blue corolla with white splashes at the petal base. Listed as hardy in some catalogues, try it as a garden bedder.

'Holly's Beauty' This superb American cultivar is part of the California Dreamers collection. The large double flowers have pink blushed white sepals and a pale lilac-blue corolla. With its trailing habit, it is excellent for hanging baskets.

'Irene Sinton' A double-flowered trailing cultivar, with blush-pink sepals and a full lilac-blue corolla with pink splashes on the petals. This fuchsia is excellent in a hanging pot or basket, although it can be prone to botrytis early in the year.

'Lilac Lustre' This is an upright bush cultivar with medium-sized double flowers with broad rose-red sepals and a powder-blue full corolla. The flower buds are very fat, almost like little red bulbs waiting to burst, adding to its beauty.

'Love's Reward' This is an aptly named cultivar with white and violet-blue single flowers, held semi-erect. The upright bushy growth and bright mid-green leaves make it ideal for growing as a small pot plant or a beautiful quarter standard.

'Sophie Louise' This is a compact and bushy cultivar with small single flowers with pink-blushed white sepals and a tight purple-blue corolla. It is extremely floriferous and makes a superb smaller standard and pot plant.

wisteria, and many darker blues that tend more toward violet. All fuchsias change colour through the life of the flower, usually starting with the most intense colour and maturing or fading as they age. Mix fuchsias with white sepals and a blue corolla with plain white fuchsias and other pale-coloured plants to make a cool collection in a shady corner. Some suitable fuchsias for this setting are 'Andrea', 'Azure Sky', 'Blue Veil', 'Carmel Blue', 'Claire Evans', 'Crystal Blue', 'Lady in Blue', 'Lillian' and 'Whickam Blue'.

Many fuchsias have either deep pink or red sepals with various shades of blue in the corolla, and these give a much warmer impression. These look their best in groups or in mixed plantings in containers with other plants with red, white, blue and even yellow flowers, to give an exciting contrast of hot and cold colours. Some good cultivars here are 'Angela Rippon', 'Blue Gown', 'Blue Lace', 'Carina Harrer', 'Happy', 'Jomam', 'Kobold', 'Lilac Lustre', 'Little Beauty' and 'Winston Churchill'.

'Lilian' This is a lovely single-flowered cultivar with pink sepals blushed white and a pastel pink-lilac corolla. The flower colours contrast beautifully with the anthers, which are a deep red before they break with pollen. It is well worth growing as a quarter standard.

'Carmel Blue' This is a vigorous shrub cultivar that will grow to a large plant quite quickly. It has attractive single flowers, with pink sepals blushed white and blue petals with a white splash at the base. The flowers lose their shape as they age and become rather open.

'Winston Churchill' This is a superb cultivar, with medium-sized double flowers with deep pink, green-tipped sepals and a lavender-blue corolla that matures to pale purple. It has upright, bushy and self-branching growth with wiry stems and narrow dark green leaves.

THE CONTAINER
garden

Fuchsias are an ideal choice for growing in containers, both on their own and as companion plants in mixed plantings. There is a tremendous range of colours to blend with every colour scheme. Large double-flowered trailing fuchsias, such as 'Blush of Dawn', 'Swingtime' or 'Haute Cuisine', display their flowers at the ideal eye level in hanging baskets. Variegated-leaf cultivars such as 'Golden Marinka' and 'Sunray' in free-standing containers add some variation of leaf colour. This chapter contains examples of different types of containers to use, tips on caring for the plants, and ideas for placing and grouping them into eye-catching displays, even co-ordinating the colours to create different moods within the garden.

Left This attractive embossed terracotta urn is standing on a brick paved patio planted with the hardy fuchsia 'Tom Thumb'. Other fuchsias and plants provide a contrasting background.

Above This ornate terracotta wall pot, hung on a brick wall in a gap created in the climbing vine, has been planted with the fuchsia 'Daisy Bell', which carries small orange and vermilion single flowers.

hanging baskets

Because the view is upward into the flower, hanging baskets are an excellent way to show off the beauty of fuchsia flowers. There are many different trailing fuchsia cultivars, ideal for baskets. You can choose to plant baskets with only one cultivar, try mixed cultivars, or combine fuchsias with companion plants – all of these can look impressive.

Right A hanging basket hanging from a wall bracket by a door, planted with fuchsias, zonal and ivy-leaf geraniums, *Hedera*, *Nepeta variegata*, trailing lobelia and *Calibrachoa*. Growing below are some colourful upright begonias.

Below A plastic container hanging from a tree branch and planted with the fuchsia cultivar 'Susan Green'. This vigorous cultivar has beautiful, classically shaped single flowers with green-tipped pale pink sepals and a coral-pink corolla.

You can use fuchsia-based hanging baskets in many places around the house and garden. The most common place for hanging baskets is suspended from strong brackets on the side of the house, beside doorways or at the corners of walls. Why not also try hanging them from strong tree branches, from the roof eaves if they have a sufficient overhang, or even within the arch of a pergola if it is high enough? The baskets can be used to brighten garages and outbuildings, or any other corners that look dull in the summer. You can also construct tiered baskets that perch on each other using special support stands, or use the type built around a single support pole.

Fuchsias are particularly good for creating a showy display in a position – say, by the front door, where you want something bright to welcome visitors – that is too shady for many of the traditional colourful bedding plants, such as geraniums and verbena, to perform well.

SINGLE-CULTIVAR BASKETS

Baskets planted up with a single cultivar will make a strong impact, and it's also very effective to use two baskets with similar shaped flowers in contrasting colours, perhaps on either side of a door. Use at least four plants in 9cm (3½in) pots in a 30cm (12in) basket, increasing to at least seven in a 40cm (16in) basket. When making the final pinching out, stop all the growing tips at the same time.

In a dark corner, a white or pastel-coloured cultivar is the best choice. Cultivars such as 'Harry Grey', 'Devonshire Dumpling', 'Natasha Sinton' or 'Walsingham' are good ones to try. In a brighter area, a more strongly coloured cultivar is better. A double-flowered red and white such as 'Swingtime' or a pink and red such as 'Seventh Heaven' are excellent choices. Strongly coloured single-flowered fuchsias such as 'Caradella', 'Marinka' or 'Postiljon' also work very well. Cultivars that have very cascading growth such as 'Cascade' or 'Put's Folly' are less suitable for single-cultivar baskets, since they flower at the end of long branches and it is difficult to make any flowers bloom in the centre of the basket. It is better to use these in mixed baskets.

MIXED BASKETS

Try to use cultivars that are fairly stiff and upright in habit, such as 'Annabel' or 'Ruth King', in the centre of the basket, and trailing or cascading cultivars around the edges. Including contrasts in foliage and flower colour helps to create a basket that is attractive from all sides. Companion plants also help to make more interesting baskets, and ivy-leaf geraniums, pendulous begonias, lobelia, *Nepeta variegata*, surfinias, verbena and many other trailing plants work really well with fuchsias in baskets to create a beautiful effect.

Right The fuchsia 'Rocket Fire' growing in a cone wicker hanging basket. The double flowers have an unusual frilled corolla with pink outer petals and purple inner petals.

FUCHSIAS FOR HANGING BASKETS

This list of cultivars is by no means exhaustive, but it does give some suggestions of rewarding cultivars to try in a hanging basket. It includes a mixture of colours, growth habits and flower sizes. The largest doubles look spectacular, but often do not produce so many flowers.

'Annabelle Stubbs'
'Ashley and Isobel'
'Auntie Jinks'
'Cascade'
'Cecile'
'Chantry Park'
'Eva Boerg'
'Golden Anniversary'
'Golden Marinka'
'Haute Cuisine'
'Harry Grey'
'Janice Ann'
'La Campanella'
'Land van Beveren'
'Postiljon'
'Purple Rain'
'Rigoletto'
'Seventh Heaven'
'Swingtime'
'Trudi Davro'
'Vanessa Jackson'
'Walsingham'
'Wendy's Beauty'

'Cascade'

'Haute Cuisine'

'Wendy's Beauty'

hanging pots

Fuchsias grown in hanging pots are a tremendously flexible solution for brightening many a dull corner. Hang them from tree branches, pergolas, under storm porches or any other places that need a floral lift. The cascading and long-lasting flowering habit of trailing fuchsias planted in hanging pots will bring a lot of pleasure throughout the entire summer.

Above 'Golden Marinka' is a beautiful variegated leaf sport from 'Marinka'. It has yellow-cream, green variegated leaves with red flowers, and looks lovely grown in a hanging pot.

Right Hanging on a branch of an apple tree is a hanging pot of the fuchsia 'Hermiena', with its white and violet single flowers.

Far right A hanging pot planted with the fuchsia cultivar 'Trudi Davro', with its double white flowers. The sepals are white in the shade but become pink when placed in the sun.

It is necessary to be clear about the differences between a hanging basket and a hanging pot. A hanging pot is made of plastic, with plastic detachable hangers and a detachable watering tray. Such a pot usually measures up to 26cm (10in) in diameter. When buying these pots, pay particular attention to the quality of the plastic hangers. If possible, buy a few spare hangers at the same time, since this is the part most liable to fail. There is a range of designs to choose from, and the most common colours are black, green or terracotta.

Plant up any small pots with a trailing fuchsia cultivar, using up to five plants depending on the pot size. Plant larger pots with a mixture of fuchsia cultivars or mixed plantings, according to your preference. After the short time needed to establish themselves, these will grow rapidly and start to flower, and from then on they will need regular watering and feeding. On very hot windy days, water them until the lower tray fills and the compost is saturated. The plant will soon use up the water in the lower tray, which acts as an extra reservoir.

PLACING HANGING POTS

Hanging pots are ideal to brighten up all sorts of odd places and neglected corners in the garden. They have the advantage of being lighter than hanging baskets, and do not need such strong supports. Suspending them in the lower branches of trees works very well, since they brighten the tree and the tree also provides them with shade. Hang them directly on smaller branches, using the plastic hook that came with the pot, or make some heavy wire hooks to fit over thicker branches, but remember to put some protection over the branch to prevent the wire cutting into the bark.

Another excellent way to display these pots is hanging from a large post, which has crosspieces placed horizontally at intervals up the post. Other good places for hanging are from pergolas, from overhanging roof eaves, or on small brackets attached to walls, sheds or fence posts. Even in a small garden, a bit of thought will reveal a number of places they can be used to add interesting colour.

VARIETIES FOR HANGING POTS

Most trailing or cascading fuchsia cultivars will work very well in hanging pots, but the best ones are those with compact and self-branching growth, especially for the smaller pot sizes, as they will make a more dense mass of flowers and foliage. In hanging pots with mixed plantings, the compact growth of the fuchsia is less important, as the other plants will fill the spaces. Double-flowered fuchsias also work very well – the smaller double types such as 'Emma Louise', 'Kon Tiki' or 'Ratatouille' are ideal. In larger pots the bigger American doubles such as 'Holly's Beauty' also work well.

Above An aged 'Bramley' apple tree giving superb dappled shade to hanging baskets and pots of fuchsias.

Below 'Princessita' is an excellent cultivar for hanging baskets or pots, with its long-lasting white and red single flowers.

FUCHSIAS FOR HANGING POTS

Cascading or trailing fuchsia cultivars look superb in hanging pots. The list below suggests some suitable fuchsia cultivars for different sized pots.

SMALLER POTS
'Ashley and Isobel'
'Auntie Jinks'
'Caradella'
'Chantry Park'
'Emma Louise'
'Golden Marinka'
'Harry Grey'
'Hermiena'
'La Campanella'
'Princessita'
'Susan Green'
'Trudy Davro'

'Harry Grey'

LARGER POTS
'Annabelle Stubbs'
'Cecile'
'Golden Anniversary'
'Holly's Beauty'
'Irene Sinton'
'Pink Marshmallow'
'Seventh Heaven'
'Wendy's Beauty'

'La Campanella'

'Irene Sinton'

other containers

Fuchsias are very adaptable plants, ideal for growing in a variety of containers, including unusual ones. Why not try something new and different? Your imagination should be the only limit. With such a wide variety of growing habits, flower colour and shape, and overall plant size, it should be possible to find a fuchsia to suit most containers.

Fuchsias are very commonly grown in the border, or in ordinary pots and hanging baskets, but why not try an unusual home for your plants in a different sort of container?

DIFFERENT SHAPES AND SIZES

Old chimney pots make excellent containers for fuchsias. The best ones for plants are those known as "bishop-type" pots, with a tall column and a wider castellated cowl at the top, which makes an excellent planting area. These look marvellous with trailing fuchsias around the edge and an upright cultivar in the centre, or you could replace the trailing fuchsias with a companion plant such as lobelia or bacopa. You can also use the smoother-shaped pots without a wider cowl at the top if you put a suitable smaller pot inside them, or stand a planted basket on top.

Try planting fuchsias in the urn-shaped containers with planting pockets on the side designed for growing herbs or strawberries. Smaller trailing varieties such as 'Auntie Jinks', 'Harry Grey', 'La Campanella' or 'Gordon Thorley' will reward you with a mound of colour throughout the summer.

Many different wall planters and pots are available these days, varying from simple plastic to terracotta (clay) with an ornate decorative back plate. They all have a flat back to hang neatly on the wall. Consider the colour of the wall and choose a flower colour that will contrast nicely, such as the

Right A chimney pot planted with the fuchsias 'Royal Velvet', a superb red and purple double, and 'Carmel Blue', a white and blue single. *Bacopa* 'Snowflake' is planted as an edging plant, to trail over the edges.

Far right An embellished lead urn looks impressive planted with 'Marinka', a red single-flowered trailing fuchsia, around the edges and the Triphylla cultivar 'Thalia' in the centre.

dark flowers of 'Janice Ann' on a white wall, or the white flowers tinged with pink of 'Harry Grey' on a red brick wall.

The simple black-plastic hanging planting tubes often used for other types of trailing summer bedding plants are a very cheap way of creating a colourful display. Plant a tube with either several plants of the same cultivar or a contrasting mixture of cultivars, insert a watering tube to reach approximately one-third of the way down in the centre, hang it up and watch it grow. You can also find rigid free-standing tubes that will make an instant fuchsia column effect.

One alternative way to grow different cultivars together is in a heavy wire stand, which holds pots at different heights. This will make an interesting display of fuchsias, and will create extra height and depth. It also helps you to see the different cultivars clearly and show off your favourite fuchsias.

The garden urn type of container, elegantly shaped and sitting on its own base or pedestal, is widely used in the garden and very useful for growing fuchsias. These urns can be made in many different materials including plastic, terracotta (clay) and stone. As with all fuchsia plantings, they look striking with smaller trailing fuchsias around the edge and an upright bushier cultivar in the middle.

Alternatively they can be planted with a mixture of plant types with fuchsias as just one component of the whole display.

USING FOUND CONTAINERS

Many other items can be adapted for use as containers with a bit of imagination, rather than throwing them away. For example, old ridge tiles, either the half-round or the V-shaped type, with some wooden feet and ends, can make interesting planters filled with fuchsias on their own or mixed with other plants. They can be placed anywhere around the garden to brighten up odd corners. Many metal items such as old coal scuttles, buckets, and even unusual items such as smelting pots can be used to plant fuchsias alone or mixed with other plants. However, be careful not to place metal containers in any position where they will be exposed to direct sun for long periods, as the metal will conduct heat quickly and cause root damage.

Wooden containers, such as wooden barrels cut in half or wooden wheelbarrows, which you can buy specifically to use as growing containers, make interesting large containers for mixed planting with fuchsias. Use the wooden barrels for planting out large standard fuchsias or trained shapes, as the weight and base area will give extra stability.

putting it all together

A collection of containers containing fuchsias alone or with other plants can be a superb sight at the peak of their flowering season. Any arrangement of containers with fuchsias in flower will look beautiful and be very good value for money, flowering continuously for a long period, attracting bees and other beneficial insects.

Below An inspired collection of containers arranged together to create a beautiful garden vista. The grouping of containers and baskets consists of fuchsias, busy Lizzies and a colourful range of other summer bedding plants.

Planning your container and flower colours beforehand is really worthwhile. Try some of the following ideas for displaying fuchsias in containers, planted out in the borders, and trained into different shapes. You may well find yourself in a fuchsia paradise, with waves of flowering fuchsias descending in tiers from each corner of your garden. Utilize different shapes, sizes and colours of fuchsias with co-ordinating companion plants. Grow them in containers of different shapes, sizes and

colours creating different moods, using mauve, blue and white colours to give a cool mood, or orange and red flowers to give an impression of warmth and heat.

ARRANGING CONTAINERS

For arrangements in corners with walls or other backdrops, create some tiers to increase the impression of height and show all the plants off really well. This can be a permanent structure, or

a temporary one with stacks of breezeblocks, block pillars or slabs, but do ensure it is strong enough to support the containers safely. Start with simple small pots at the front and larger pots or containers behind, then add more pots and containers on the tiers behind this. Setting a standard fuchsia at the back will raise the height still further.

For a free-standing display in the centre of an area of lawn or paving, follow a similar design, but check that you have considered the full 360-degree aspect to give an equally good view from any side. These central displays can look very effective in paved areas or on surfaces covered with decorative chippings of different colours and textures.

PLACING POTS

Tiered staging set against a wall is a good way to display pot fuchsias, especially bonsai fuchsias. Another excellent way to show them off is on a post set in the ground, with crosspieces alternating at 90 degrees to each other, all the way up the post. On the end of each crosspiece fix a plastic pot, and then drop in fuchsias in pots of the same size to create a pillar of fuchsia flowers. If you keep some spare plants in the same-sized pots, you can exchange any fuchsias that are not flowering well.

Various types of commercial pot stands are available, varying from the simplest wire ring stand on a single leg that pushes into the soil, through those with three legs and a base, to more ornate cast iron versions, including semi-circular étagères. For specimen plants you can obtain stone or cast concrete pillars or stands with matching pots that really display the plant well. These look splendid topped with specimen fuchsias on either side of a gate. There are also ornate cast iron pot stands that attach to a wall, or you can fix pot supports to a trellis or wood framework and fill them with fuchsias to make a wonderful display.

DISPLAYING HANGING BASKETS

Apart from fixing hanging baskets or pots to tree branches or wall brackets, an excellent way of displaying them is from a pergola, which allows you to walk underneath and see the beauty of the flowers from the best angle. This is especially good for the large double-flowered fuchsias. The other advantage of a pergola is that it is easy to add shade netting over the top of the pergola in very hot spells of weather, creating the additional shade that fuchsias love. Try placing standards and pots within the pergola, all along the edges, to create the visual effect of a tunnel of fuchsias.

You can also buy stands that allow you to place baskets of decreasing sizes on top of one another, and when planted with trailing fuchsias, begonias and geraniums these can look superb, forming a cascading fountain of colour.

Left A lovely weathered terracotta (clay) pot planted with the hardy fuchsia cultivar 'Alice Hoffman'. The semi-double to double flower has dark cerise sepals and a cerise-veined, fluffy white corolla, and the foliage – especially at the growing tips – is an attractive bronzy green. Around it are growing regal and zonal geraniums.

Below An antique mangle stand forms the framework for an attractive display against an old brick wall. Mixed containers filled with fuchsias, begonias, lobelia and other flowering plants are enveloping and trailing over the framework to give a wonderful cascade of colour.

THE INDOOR
garden

Fuchsias grown inside the house can be striking flowering plants, although special care is necessary to protect them from the dry atmosphere in centrally heated modern houses. A conservatory is an excellent place to grow and enjoy fuchsias intermingled with other tender plants, especially scented ones, since scent is a quality fuchsias lack. A greenhouse, an important resource for any serious gardener, is ideal for growing and propagating fuchsias, and is essential for overwintering larger trained structures such as standards or fans.

In areas of the world with very hot, dry summer conditions, a shadehouse is almost a requirement for the serious fuchsia grower to maintain the cooler, more humid conditions they love.

Left A display of many different fuchsia cultivars in a greenhouse on a staging table. Notice the arrangement of heights of the different plants, giving a tiered effect.

Above A hanging basket, suspended from the greenhouse roof, planted with the cultivar 'Laura', a strong-growing, spreading single-flowered fuchsia with a light orange tube and sepals, and a reddish-orange corolla.

fuchsias inside a house

During the latter half of the 19th century, when fuchsias first became popular, they were a common sight growing indoors as decorative house plants. The imported species such as *F. coccinea* and the new hybrids grown as specimen house plants were very expensive at that time and only available to the wealthy gardener.

Right 'Tom West' is a fuchsia grown for its beautiful green-cream and cerise foliage. This example is grown indoors; the colours intensify with more light. The small single flowers are red and purple.

Below The fuchsias 'Bland's New Striped' and 'Claire de Lune' growing as colourful house plants.

Most houses in the latter part of the 19th century were rather cold and damp, conditions in which fuchsias thrive. Modern houses are often double-glazed, centrally heated and rather dry inside and so do not offer advantageous conditions to grow fuchsias as house plants. Fuchsias that have been growing well outside often respond by dropping their flower buds and sometimes their leaves when moved inside, mainly due to the change in humidity and light levels. However, if you put some effort into providing the right conditions and adjusting plants to the new growing conditions while they are still small, fuchsias can be successfully grown in the house.

REQUIREMENTS FOR INDOOR FUCHSIAS

The first requirement for fuchsias grown as house plants is a boost in humidity. Stand the plants on trays of gravel, pebbles or water-retaining fired clay particles, with water in the bottom of the trays, but making sure the water level is below the base of the pots. Take care that the trays used do not leak, to prevent water damage to furniture.

The next requirement for indoor fuchsias is light. Fuchsias need good light to grow well, but not too much direct sunlight when grown in a house. Choose a windowsill that receives only early or late sun, and do not forget to turn the plants frequently. During the winter, in locations at latitudes more than 40° north or south, move the plants to where they will receive as much sunlight as possible, because of the shorter days and lower intensity of the sun.

GROWING FUCHSIAS INDOORS

There are two main ways to grow indoor fuchsias. For the first method, root a cutting in a small propagator indoors – a pot-type propagator is ideal.

Acclimatize the cutting gradually to indoor conditions by slowly increasing the amount of ventilation after rooting until it is in the open indoor atmosphere. Grow on, training as a shrub and later, with more experience, you can try training other shapes.

The second method is to bring in a plant that has been growing in a pot outside. Choose a plant that is not in flower, or is just coming into bud; keep it on the dry side by watering sparsely, and grow it in a position that is not too high in humidity for two to three weeks. Move the plant indoors and place it on a gravel tray. Mist it frequently with water in the first week indoors, while gradually increasing the watering. After two weeks, the plant will have adjusted to inside conditions.

CULTIVARS TO CHOOSE

Choose short-jointed self-branching cultivars if possible, since the lower light levels indoors will cause an increase in the internodal stem length. In general, hardy cultivars seem to tolerate indoor conditions quite well, and single-flowered cultivars manage better than doubles. If you would like to try a double, use a small-flowered one as it has more chance of keeping its flowers. When growing a group of plants together, try to vary the size and elevation to create interest, or use a small trained shape such as a miniature standard, fan or pillar. Use cultivars that give an interesting variation in flower colour, and those with variegated foliage, such as 'Tom West', to add different leaf colours.

FUCHSIAS FOR GROWING INDOORS
The following is a list of cultivars which have been noted as being suitable for growing indoors.

'Baby Chang'
'Bambini'
'Chang'
'Display'
'Dollar Princess'
'Heidi Ann'
'Little Beauty'
'Minirose'
'Sandboy'
'Tom West'

'Dollar Princess'

Above Planted in an unusual smelting pot, together with a golden-leafed helichrysum, 'Kolding Perle' is a single-flowered fuchsia with waxy white sepals and a pink cerise corolla. This cultivar originated from Denmark.

Left Inside the house around the Christmas tree, the fuchsia 'Alice Hoffman' sits in a wicker basket decorated as a special gift grouped among the other Christmas presents.

conservatory fuchsias

A conservatory is an area of transition between the house and the garden. It is often used as both an extension of the living room and a space for growing plants. It is ideal for growing new fuchsias and for overwintering fuchsias and other plants, creating a warm and light atmosphere which is very enjoyable to sit and relax in on a cold day.

Right Multiple plants of 'Eva Boerg' planted in a flower tower, growing in a conservatory. 'Eva Boerg' is a trailing fuchsia with semi-double flowers with pink-white sepals and a pinkish-purple corolla.

Below A conservatory filled with tropical foliage plants and fuchsias in terracotta (clay) pots supported by an ornamental plant stand.

The word "conservatory" originates from the Italian *conservato* ("stored" or "preserved") combined with the Latin suffix *-ory* ("a place for"), and originally meant a place for storing food. Conservatories as we know them today were first built by wealthy gardeners who wished to grow the exotic and unusual specimens discovered in warmer regions by plant hunters. The costs of glass and winter heating originally made them prohibitive for all but the wealthiest families, but the production of cheaper glass and other materials gradually made them more accessible. In the modern age, construction in steel-reinforced PVC or hardwood, with double-glazed glass units, combined with advances such as solar reflecting and self-cleaning glass and under-floor heating, has made the modern conservatory a comfortable extension to the living space. Fuchsias will grow very well there providing you can keep up sufficient local humidity and make sure the inside is cool enough in the summer. If you feel comfortable in the conservatory, the fuchsias will probably be comfortable as well.

CONDITIONS AND PLANTING IDEAS

The humidity of the atmosphere is very important. It will be beneficial to use waterproof trays containing wet gravel, expanded clay beads or similar media on the floor and underneath the plants, combined with spray misting. Therefore it is obviously a good idea to use robust furnishings and to keep anything that is likely to be spoiled by water away from the fuchsias. Similarly, the floor around them should be easy to clean as some dead leaves and flowers are bound to fall on the floor.

Combinations of larger plants standing on the floor, on stands, on shelving or hanging from supports are useful to make an attractive display of fuchsias,

showing their flowers to the best advantage.
The conservatory will extend the flowering period
of the fuchsias considerably, and with some
staggering of the time of pruning, it is possible
to have fuchsias in flower for most of the year.

Fuchsias combined with other plants in the
conservatory can make interesting combinations
and ensure interest all the year round. Some good
companion plants are climbers such as *Jasminum
polyanthum,* bougainvillea and plumbago, or shrubs
such as *Hoya carnosta* (wax plant), *Gardenia
jasminoides* and citrus. Use a mixture of fuchsias –
singles, doubles, trailing and trained shapes like
standards – to fit in with the surrounding plants.
If the conservatory is very sunny, it will need blinds
and good ventilation to prevent it becoming too hot
in the summer; indeed, in any continuous hot spells
of weather, it is worth giving the tenderest of plants
a breather outside in a shady position.

CARING FOR CONSERVATORY FUCHSIAS

In a conservatory, the aim is to keep plants
flowering throughout the year, so prune fuchsias
in a similar way to plants growing in frost-free
equatorial or tropical regions. Conservatory fuchsias
need more gentle and partial pruning, mainly to
shape and tidy them, leaving budding shoots intact
to maintain flowering. Unglazed terracotta (clay)
pots are the best to use since they allow the
compost (soil mix) to breathe, helping to cool

the roots. This breathing also helps to create
more humidity around the plant.

Plants are best introduced into the conservatory
in the autumn or winter so that they have a chance
to acclimatize to the conditions before the stress
of the summer heat. You can put either new young
plants or old plants that have been cut back in the
conservatory, but ensure any pests and diseases
are eradicated before moving them in. Avoid using
insecticides, as these chemicals should not be
allowed to enter the house. Turn the plants through
90 degrees every so often to prevent them leaning
over toward the light, and feed them regularly or
use a slow-release fertilizer in the compost.

FUCHSIAS FOR CONSERVATORIES
Many fuchsia cultivars will grow well in a
conservatory. Those listed here are smaller-
flowered cultivars that will bloom well.

'Bambini'
'Brutus'
'Display'
'Dollar Princess'
'Heidi Ann'
'Little Jewel'
'Minirose'
'Nellie Nuttall'
'Sandboy'

'Nellie Nuttall'

Above left Fuchsia
'Happy Wedding Day'
is an Australian white
double-flowered cultivar
with lax growth. It is
seen here growing with
busy Lizzies among ferns
in a conservatory.

Above 'Autumnale'
growing in a moss-
lined basket hanging in
a conservatory. It is a
spreading fuchsia grown
mainly for its beautiful
dark red, salmon and
yellow-splashed foliage.

greenhouse fuchsias

A greenhouse is more than a luxury – it is an essential piece of equipment for serious fuchsia growers whose gardens experience freezing temperatures in the winter. You will find it invaluable for storing and preserving plants, for keeping them growing over the winter period, and for propagating new stock.

Right The author's greenhouse, with six large roof-vents giving excellent ventilation. The large double doors allow easy movement of large plants in and out.

Below A commercial greenhouse filled with fuchsias on staging, as well as fuchsia hanging pots suspended from part of the roof structure.

A greenhouse is a wonderful resource for the gardener – indeed, it is almost essential for the really keen fuchsia grower in colder winter climates. It makes it possible to overwinter some of the larger trained shapes such as fans, pyramids and standards, propagate new plants, and even grow a climbing fuchsia if you wish.

The greenhouse extends the growing season by creating a microclimate, insulating the fuchsias from the outside conditions. Beware of overheating the greenhouse in the winter, though, since the result will be rather long spindly growth and it is better to keep your plants as compact and strong as possible.

TYPES OF GREENHOUSE

There are many possible types and constructions of greenhouse. You can choose from aluminium or wood, glass or plastic, brick sides or glass down to the ground. If you are going to use your greenhouse for growing fuchsias, make sure yours is at least 2.9m x 2.2m (10ft x 7ft), preferably bigger if you have the space. Greenhouses with sufficient height for you to stand upright close to the edges are the best. If you live in an area subject to strong winds, choose one with a heavyweight frame and a good glazing system. Plastic glazing is an alternative, especially the twin-wall type, which gives better insulation in the winter and more heat protection in the summer. Add additional ventilation in the form of top vents and louvres, and ensure that at least one or two of the top vents can be opened manually, preferably with a screw thread.

POSITION OF THE GREENHOUSE

Ideally, the greenhouse should run from north to south lengthwise, as this will give the most even distribution of sun. If possible, arrange for the

minimum natural shade in the winter, and some shade from a deciduous tree in the summer. Avoid placing it in a dip, which may flood in heavy rain in the winter, and also try to avoid the windiest parts of the garden. Different bases are available, but the best are built from bricks or blocks, and paved internally with concrete slabs or brick. Part of the floor could also be a layer of gravel on weed-suppression matting.

STAGING

You will need something to stand your plants on in the greenhouse. Most manufacturers will supply staging in aluminium, with a choice of open slats or aluminium trays, or you can build your own in wood. Ensure the staging is at a comfortable working height, and can easily be removed if you want the floor area for larger plants.

SHADING

In the spring and summer, shading is essential to protect the plants from too much direct sun and help to keep the temperature down. There are various solutions: the simplest is to paint white shading on the outside of the glass, and the best solution is to fit roller blinds with shade netting on the outside. Whatever you use, it will make the greenhouse much cooler.

GROWING PLANTS

There is a temptation, when you buy a splendid new greenhouse, to fill it up by purchasing new plants, accepting gifts from friends, or propagating far too many plants. Try to avoid doing this, unless you know you can give many of your plants away in the early spring. As a rule of thumb, the greenhouse should be maximum one-half full in the winter. One way to make yourself adhere to this rule is to partition off about one-third of the space with a plastic sheet, and only heat this section in the winter.

The heated greenhouse allows you to grow cultivars and species that are more tender and difficult to grow. Examples of these tender species are *F. venusta*, a beautiful climbing fuchsia with orange-red flowers and wine-red stems, and *F. triphylla*, the parent of the modern Triphylla hybrids, which is small-growing in cultivation, with orange-red flowers. Some tender cultivars are quite difficult to overwinter and grow better in a heated greenhouse. Some such cultivars are 'Citation', a beautiful American single fuchsia with rose-pink sepals and a white flared saucer-shaped corolla, and 'Constellation', an American white double.

Another good use for the greenhouse is to bring containers into flower before moving them outside for your summer display (you can then overwinter them under cover if you wish).

Above A basket hanging from the greenhouse roof, planted with the lovely fuchsia, 'Swingtime'.

Below left A collection of small fuchsia plants stand on a gravel bed in the autumn. Centre front is 'Tom West'.

Below A selection of trained standards and fan fuchsias growing in a commercial greenhouse.

Above Hanging baskets of fuchsias growing in a commercial greenhouse, suspended from a support rail in the roof. Notice the green shading material fixed in the roof space.

Right A collection of fuchsia standards growing in a greenhouse over the winter. They were cut back in the autumn, started to grow again and are ticking over in green leaf.

EARLY SPRING

In early spring, as the outside temperatures start to rise and the day length increases, the conditions inside the greenhouse promote rapid fuchsia growth. Make sure that you keep the plants well spaced out, turn them regularly, and pinch out the growth and pot them on as necessary. Conditions can be quite challenging at this time of year, as on bright sunny days the temperature can rise to over 25°C (77°F), yet overnight frosts are still possible. It is best to keep the greenhouse well ventilated on sunny days, and try to water or mist in the mornings, so that the plants do not sit in too much moisture overnight. When the days are warm enough and free of cold winds, the plants will benefit from a spell outside, hardening up the soft growth and keeping them growing in a compact way.

Early to mid-spring is a good time to start planting up hanging baskets, pots and containers, as many fuchsias and companion plants start to become available from nurseries and garden centres. For the next few weeks, before you move them outside, control the watering in the greenhouse, keeping them on the dry side, so they will fill the compost (soil mix) with new roots. They will make plenty of growth and will already be in flower when moved outside in the late spring.

LATE SPRING

As the sun becomes brighter and the days longer, light shading will be necessary on the greenhouse roof and the sides receiving direct sun to prevent scorching of the young growth. Again, continue to move plants outside on suitable days to continue the hardening-up process and ensure the plants acclimatize to the outside conditions before you move them out for good. Space is often at a premium in the greenhouse at this time of year and you may need to move some plants outside permanently before they are completely ready. If so, be prepared to protect them with fleece if there is a late frost. Plant up any remaining baskets and containers with your chosen plants, and add full shading to the greenhouse glass if the weather gets very warm.

SUMMER

Throughout the summer months, fuchsias are better growing outside, but if you wish to continue growing some plants inside, ensure that you use maximum ventilation at all times, even to the extent of removing some glass panes and replacing them with fine netting. If you are growing plants for

exhibition, the same netting can be placed over all the vents and a detachable piece over the doors, as this will help to keep bees and other insects out and prevent damage and marking of the flowers. Keep the floor and any gravel trays wet to increase the humidity – this will also help to cool the greenhouse, but ensure fuchsias are not sitting in water.

AUTUMN

During the late summer and early autumn, empty the greenhouse completely, clean all the glass, replacing any panes which were removed during the summer, sterilize all the benching and any other structures and check the heaters are working properly. Make sure that the whole structure is sound, replacing any cracked glass, and clean and if necessary lubricate the door slides or hinges and the vent openers. Now the greenhouse will be ready for its winter storage duties once more.

WINTER

Depending on the temperature you maintain through the winter months, the greenhouse can be used either to protect dormant plants, or to keep plants ticking over in green leaf. It is better not to overheat, since this will promote more rapid growth, which will become straggly and drawn

owing to the low light levels in winter. A minimum temperature of 5°C (41°F) is ideal, not using too much energy, but protecting even the Triphylla hybrids. Keep the plants that are still in green leaf quite dry through the winter, removing any damaged or dying leaves, and give the greenhouse some ventilation on all but the coldest days. As the days start to lengthen in spring, the plants in green leaf will start to grow fresh green growth, which is ideal for early-season cuttings. It is important to turn the plants regularly to prevent them becoming one-sided, and to pinch them out to encourage bushiness, increasing the number of potential flowering shoots.

Above left A large plant of the hardy cultivar 'Hawkshead' growing in a greenhouse. It has white single flowers, which stay white in the sun, and small bright green leaves.

Above A staging table full of fuchsia plants in a commercial greenhouse, labelled and placed in groups ready for eager customers to buy. It is easy to find this environment very inspiring and tempting, but do not buy more than you can grow.

Left These fuchsias are overwintering on the floor of the greenhouse. They have been cut back in the autumn, and are now ticking over in green leaf.

shadehouse fuchsias

In hotter climates, a shadehouse is an essential item to ensure fuchsias will thrive through the heat of the summer months. In areas where the summer temperatures regularly reach the high 30s in Celsius (over 100°F), such as Australia, New Zealand and the southern United States, fuchsias in pots will not easily survive outside in the garden.

A shadehouse creates ideal natural growing conditions for fuchsias and helps to preserve the colour of any white-flowered varieties that tend to become pink in the sun.

In the height of the summer, it is also possible to provide shading for some plants growing in the ground outside the shadehouse by using netting on poles. Very keen fuchsia growers and exhibitors in cooler parts of the world also sometimes use shadehouses in the summer to reduce the damage from wind and rain, when a greenhouse might be too hot and bright.

Below A view through the doorway of a shadehouse in midsummer. Inside are many pot-grown fuchsias in flower growing on beds of moist gravel. Note the green shading material on the sides and roof.

TYPES OF SHADEHOUSE

The oldest kind of shadehouse, which is still used in some parts of the world, is the lath house. The simplest lath house is constructed as a box frame with strong corner posts and crosspieces, made large enough to stand up and work in comfortably. Cover the roof with thin strips of wood (lath), typically 2.5–3 cm (1–1¼in) wide, spaced to give an equal gap between each one. The sides may also be covered in a similar way. An interesting alternative construction once used in California is a roof made from close-spaced old fluorescent tubes.

The modern shadehouse is made from a tubular frame, which is easily erected and covered with polypropylene shade netting, usually green, which can be bought in a range of sun-shading densities, although 50 per cent shading is the most common. It is also possible to make a wooden frame and cover it with shade netting, or to erect a pergola that can be shaded in the hottest parts of the year.

There is plenty of choice of materials for the floor, but remember it needs to be able to drain in times of heavy rain, so use sloped paving, and if gravel is used, use a porous material such as weed suppression matting.

ADVANTAGES OF SHADEHOUSES
Apart from their obvious sun-shading qualities, shadehouses provide some protection from the wind, helping to stop plants from being blown over. Those made of shade netting also break up heavy drops of rain into a fine mist that fuchsias love. Hot places in the world may not get much rain, but when it does rain, it is often torrential, so this is a real extra benefit. Shadehouses do not provide

anything but the lightest protection from frost, so do not move any plants into them until all danger of frost is past. For exhibitors, another benefit is to limit the access of bees, which can damage and mark the flowers trying to reach the nectar.

GROWING FUCHSIAS IN A SHADEHOUSE
Grow pot plants free-standing on the floor in the shadehouse, providing that there is side protection from the wind. Taller structures such as standards need support, for example tying them to wires strung along one side of the house. Suspend hanging baskets and pots from the roof, but be aware that this will create extra shade for any plants below them.

Visiting an enthusiast's shadehouse for the first time can be an impressive experience. You feel the change in temperature and humidity as you walk in; then comes the enthralling sight of rows of pot plants, standards and baskets with flowers of different shapes, sizes and colours. The shadehouse allows the keen gardener to grow more unusual cultivars, so you will perhaps spot some fuchsias that are rarely grown in your area.

Above A magnificent fuchsia fan growing in a shadehouse, surrounded by other fuchsias in pots. This cultivar is 'Waveney Gem', a medium-sized single-flowered fuchsia with white sepals and a mauve corolla flushed with pink. It has quite light green foliage, and grows as a vigorous lax bush. It is very adaptable, and excels as a basket plant, a small standard or a fan.

GARDENING
techniques

Growing fuchsias is an exciting and rewarding pastime. There are so many colours, shapes and sizes of flowers and types of growth to choose from. Some fuchsias are hardy and can be grown as permanent shrubs. This chapter contains tips and techniques for planting and growing both hardy and the more tender varieties. There is advice about choosing and buying fuchsia cultivars, propagating them, and training them into beautiful shapes such as standards. Information about the growing media, and their suitability for growing fuchsias, is followed by practical advice on the planting of large containers and hanging baskets. These useful hints will be of value to anyone interested in growing these beautiful plants.

Left You do not need many specialist tools to grow fuchsias. Simple basic garden tools such as a pair of secateurs, a selection of plant pots and labels, a garden trowel and a hoe will suffice.

Above A large terracotta (clay) pot surrounded by fuchsias, geraniums and other companion plants ready for planting. This picture is from the start of a planting sequence, shown in full within this chapter.

selecting and buying fuchsias

One of the most enjoyable parts of growing fuchsias as a hobby is the selection of new cultivars. The inspiration can come from cultivars in other people's gardens, or from looking at nursery catalogues. There is a tremendous sense of excitement in waiting for those first buds of your new cultivars to open and reveal the hidden inner flower secrets.

A fuchsia enthusiast should try to support the specialist fuchsia nurseries as much as possible, since this will help to keep a large variety of unusual cultivars in cultivation. The owners are usually enthusiasts themselves and will often be able to give very useful help and advice with problems you have, or suggestions of cultivars.

Below 'Display' is an excellent hardy cultivar for a beginner. It is very adaptable in its growth and is easy to grow as a standard or pyramid. It has dark foliage and almost self-coloured pink flowers with a flared corolla.

ORDERING FUCHSIAS
Browse the catalogues and decide on the cultivars you want to try. Most of the specialist fuchsia nurseries will accept orders for rooted cuttings or plants in small pots to be supplied in the late winter or early spring, and this is the best way to be sure you get the cultivars you want. Getting together with friends and ordering together is one way to make this more economically viable.

Some growers will send an order by post, and while this is probably a good solution if you live a long way from the nursery, the best way to ensure that you start with healthy plants is to collect them yourself. Expect to come away with more plants than you ordered, though!

WHAT TO LOOK FOR
The first thing to do is to look carefully at the plant you are thinking of buying.
- Does it look strong and healthy?
- Are there any signs of disease?
- Is the growth even and balanced?

choosing plants for cuttings

1 Look for plants with shoots pinched out evenly and growing in a balanced way. Try to choose plants not recently stopped with growing tips.

2 This is an ideal shoot to take a tip cutting from. It is healthy, growing strongly and evenly, and there is a pair of leaves and a small growing tip.

potting up standard cuttings

1 Choose cuttings with balanced even growth to grow on as a standard. You can see the well-developed and healthy root systems.

2 Pot up into 6cm (2½in) pots and keep them separate from your other plants, so you remember not to pinch out the tops.

Next, look at the plant from above.
- Are the leaves growing evenly?
- Are the side shoots growing evenly? Often when the leaves are bigger on one side of the plant, the side shoots will be stronger as well.

If you want to take cuttings from the plant when you get home, pick one that has not recently been stopped. If you are considering growing a standard, look for an unstopped plant or a rooted cutting that is growing strongly, with a straight stem.

CARE OF NEW PLANTS

When you have bought rooted cuttings or small plants from a nursery early in the season, remember they have probably been growing in more heat than you will be able to provide. If you want to take cuttings from them, do so straight away, as these will go directly into your propagator and not experience any check in growth. When you bring new plants into your greenhouse, try to place them in the warmest position you can find and gradually get them used to the growing conditions over about a week. When they are ready for potting up or potting on, move them into the next size pot and settle them in with an overhead spray, but do not soak the compost.

LARGER PLANTS

If you do not have the facilities to raise small plants in a greenhouse early in the season, simply buy larger plants later in the season for growing on outside, following the previous guidelines for stopping and potting on.

potting up rooted cuttings

1 Pot up a rooted fuchsia cutting in a 6cm (2½in) pot, taking care not to disturb or damage the fine root system.

2 Water the fuchsia cutting in its new pot with a fine rose or an overhead spray. Use just enough water to settle the cutting in its pot.

potting up mail-order plants

1 Remove the rooted fuchsia cuttings in their protective transparent cells from the delivery box sent through the post.

2 Open the protective plastic package, showing the rooted cuttings with the labels secured with elastic bands around the root ball.

3 Remove the elastic band and label from the plant root ball and place in a suitable-size small pot such as a 6cm (2½in). Write a plastic plant label with the cultivar name at the same time.

4 Complete the potting-up of the cutting by gently adding compost (soil mix) and tapping the pot to settle the contents. This cultivar is the Triphylla 'Chantry Park'.

5 Water the cuttings into their pots, using an overhead spray. Do not overwater at this time, but use enough water to settle and moisten the compost, allowing the roots to grow.

composts and feeds

The quality of the compost (soil mix) used in containers is very important if you want to get the best out of the plants you buy. It is the anchor for the roots and the reservoir for water and plant nutrients. Its structure is equally important, as this will allow the passage of air, vital for the health of the roots.

There are many types of commercial potting compost (soil mix) used both in gardens and indoors. They are prepared from various base materials such as loam, moss peat, coir (from coconut husks), composted bark and, more recently, composted green waste. Additives are used to improve wetting, open the texture and improve the drainage. Fuchsias additionally benefit from the addition of extra material, such as grit and vermiculite or perlite, to open up the texture of the compost and improve the drainage.

TYPES OF COMPOST

Lawrence and Newell, two scientists at the John Innes Institute, developed the first standardized and reproducible potting compost during the 1930s. These mixes are known as John Innes formula composts, and consist of seven parts loam, three parts peat and two parts gritty sand (by volume)

with increasing amounts of fertilizer to make the number one, two and three grades.

Soil-less compost (growing medium) was developed at the University of California, and is known as UC compost. It consists of 75 per cent sphagnum moss peat and 25 per cent coarse sand with added fertilizers. There have been many variations on this mixture, including the use of other additives such as vermiculite and water-retention granules. However, nowadays there is a concern about the unsustainable use of sphagnum moss peat, which can potentially destroy sites of special scientific interest. The search for substitutes has resulted in various alternatives such as coir, composted bark and, more recently, composted recycled green waste.

COMPOST FOR FUCHSIAS

Fuchsias will grow well in most good quality general-purpose composts. They prefer an open free-draining mixture, obtained by using additives as described below. In terracotta (clay) pots, mixes containing 50 per cent or more loam are very suitable. For plastic pots, the soil-free types work well, although the use of up to 20 per cent loam can be beneficial.

ADDITIVES

Additives are non-fertilizing materials mixed into the compost before use. Vermiculite, a thermally expanded mica, and perlite, another expanded mineral, open up the texture, and improve the drainage and water-retention abilities of the compost. Use them at a ratio of about one part vermiculite or perlite to six parts compost (by volume). Coarse sand and grit function purely as structure and drainage aids, but they will also add some weight to the compost mix, improving the

Below Some different composts (soil mixes) and additives. At the back from left to right are: peat-free multi-purpose compost, loam-based compost and moss peat. At the front from left to right are: water retention granules, vermiculite and coarse grit.

stability of pot plants, especially when they dry out. Use them at a ratio of about one volume part to six volume parts compost. When using multiple additives together, reduce the proportions accordingly. Water retention gel has become very popular mixed in with compost in hanging baskets, which often dry out very quickly. It will both improve the retention of water in the basket, and make re-wetting dry compost easier.

FERTILIZERS AND FEEDS

Fertilizers are solid materials mixed into the compost before use. Commercial compost normally contains sufficient fertilizer for a few months of growing. Feeds are liquid fertilizers, normally a liquid concentrate or soluble powder applied during watering or sprayed on as a foliar feed. Fuchsias, like all plants, need three major elements: nitrogen (N), phosphorus (P) and potassium (K) (commonly known as potash from its horticultural origin in wood ash). Nitrogen promotes leafy growth, phosphorus is needed for the roots,

and potash promotes hardening of the wood, and flower and fruit formation. In addition, there are a number of trace elements and minor components needed for healthy growth of the plants. Fertilizers are labelled with their N:P:K contents, measured in weight per cent. For example, a high-nitrogen feed could be 30:15:15, a balanced feed would be 20:20:20 and a high-potash feed 15:15:30.

One simple option is to use slow-release fertilizer granules. These contain concentrated fertilizer encapsulated in a polymer shell, which will not start to release the fertilizer until the compost reaches a certain temperature. The rate of release is dependent on the temperature and, to an extent, the moisture content. Alternatively, use liquid concentrate or soluble powder fertilizers mixed with water to give the correct strength. Fuchsias like a high-nitrogen feed early in the season, and a balanced feed for the rest of the season. You can use a high-potash feed at flowering time, preferably alternated with a balanced feed. Regular, weak solutions are better than infrequent, strong ones.

Above Some fertilizers and equipment used for growing fuchsias in the greenhouse, including a hand pressure sprayer, liquid fertilizer concentrate, slow-release fertilizer granules and a small watering can. In the background are overwintered fuchsia cuttings potted up and growing in 6cm (2½in) pots.

hybridization techniques

Fuchsia hybridizers have produced more than 10,000 recorded cultivars, of which perhaps 5,000 or more are still in cultivation around the world. A whole range of fuchsia flower colours exists, with only a yellow and a deep royal blue evading the plant breeders so far, but it is only a matter of time until someone succeeds.

Only the species fuchsia will grow true from seed, and the creation of modern cultivars is by hybridization of two cultivars and growing on the resultant seed. If a seedling looks promising enough to be sold as a new commercial cultivar, the new plants for sale are then produced by vegetative propagation (cuttings). A more natural mutation of fuchsias, arising from "sporting", has produced many more new fuchsias, including variegated-leaf cultivars such as 'Golden Marinka' from 'Marinka', and cultivars with different flower colours, such as 'Lady Thumb' and 'Son of Thumb' from 'Tom Thumb'. The range of fuchsias available to buy is now quite extensive.

Below The fuchsia 'Alan Titchmarsh' is named after a famous British gardening celebrity. This bush plant has semi-double flowers with rose sepals and a pale lilac-pink corolla.

PARTS OF THE FUCHSIA FLOWER
The fuchsia flower is formed of insect-attracting parts (including the colourful sepals and petals) and reproductive parts.

pedicel

ovary

tube

sepal

petal (collectively, all the petals form the corolla)

filament
anther } stamen

style } + ovary
stigma } = pistil

HISTORY OF HYBRIDIZATION
Since gardeners began their attempts at hybridization early in the 19th century, many different fuchsias have been produced with varying shapes and sizes of leaf and flower and with new flower colours. After the surge of new cultivars in the 19th century, fuchsias lost some of their popularity in the early part of the 20th century, but interest was revived by the formation of national fuchsia societies and the realization that the fuchsia was not just a greenhouse plant, but could also be grown in the garden as a hardy shrub.

In the 1930s a group of enthusiasts from the recently formed British Fuchsia Society collected 100 of the best cultivars available in Europe and took them to California at the request of the American Fuchsia Society. American growers then applied scientific methods to further hybridization and soon started to produce new cultivars with unusual colour combinations, as well as the range of large double-flowered fuchsias for which they are famous. In Europe, the focus was more on producing hardy cultivars with a better range of flower colours and sizes. In the last decade, there has been a huge increase in the production of cultivars with new and exciting flower colours and shapes.

MAKING YOUR OWN HYBRID

If you wish to produce a new fuchsia, you must first make a selected hybridization cross between two cultivars or species, or a combination of the two. The first step is to select the two separate cultivars or species to use as the pollen parent and the seed parent. Experienced hybridizers have their preferences for these, knowing the previous parentage of cultivars and the viability of their seed production. For example, the cultivars 'La Campanella' and 'String of Pearls' have been used quite extensively as seed parents. It's best to do some research, by consulting reference books and talking to other growers, before you make your choice.

GROWING ON HYBRID SEEDLINGS

Once your hybridized seeds have germinated – which may take up to six weeks, so be patient – let them grow until they are large enough to handle. Prick them out (holding them by the leaves, to avoid damaging the stems or roots) into individual pots and grow them on without stopping, potting on as necessary, or in the summer you can plant them out into a trial bed. Judge the growth habit and the flower as objectively as you can, if possible bringing in some other growers to help with the assessment.

Take cuttings from the best candidates and try growing them for a few more years. If you have anything that looks really interesting, contact one of your local fuchsia nurseries, as the growers are always interested in new cultivars.

hybridizing fuchsia plants

1 Pop open a flower bud one or two days before it would normally open.

2 Emasculate the flower by carefully cutting away all the anthers (pollen-bearing organs) with scissors.

3 Protect the flower from chance pollination with a fine muslin (cheesecloth) or polythene bag.

4 Pollinate the stigma by transferring pollen from the anthers of the selected male parent flower. Reseal in the protective bag and label. Remove the bag in 5 to 6 days when the flower has died. Allow the seed berry to form and ripen.

collecting and planting seeds

1 Carefully squash the ripe berry in a small dish of water.

2 Break up the flesh as much as possible in the water, releasing the seeds.

3 Filter the mixture through a fine sieve (strainer), washing through the berry debris with the water.

4 Carefully pick out the seeds and remove on to a paper towel.

5 Transfer the seeds into a pot or tray of good quality seed compost, pressing them into the surface. Sow a maximum of 50 seeds in a 9cm (3½in) half pot.

6 Place a transparent plastic or glass cover on the pot and germinate at 15.5–18°C (60–65°F).

propagating fuchsias

Taking cuttings is a really simple and rewarding way of propagating fuchsias to increase or replace stock. The stock of a specific fuchsia cultivar can only be increased in this way; plants propagated from collected seed will not come true except for the fuchsia species, although – who knows – you may grow an interesting new cultivar from seed.

You can take cuttings at almost any time of the year, using different techniques. Take soft cuttings in the late winter and spring; semi-ripe cuttings in the summer; and woody cuttings in the autumn. It is also possible to take soft cuttings in the autumn by cutting back plants in the late summer and allowing them to shoot again. Ensure all cutting material used is short-jointed and free from any disease or infestation, and choose only material from strong and healthy growing plants.

SOFT CUTTINGS

Depending on your location, climate and greenhouse conditions, take soft cuttings in the late winter or spring when plants are growing strongly.

Different parts of the shoot can be used as cuttings, but it's always best to use a tip cutting, if you have enough material. The tip cutting contains the highest concentration of natural growth hormones and it will root more quickly. It also gives a more symmetrical cutting, with the flexibility to be trained and grown on in different ways.

Before you start, ensure the parent plant is well watered and the growth is turgid. Look for growing tips where the growth is symmetrical, and cut just below a node with a razor-sharp knife to give a cutting with two sets of leaves and a growing tip. Try to avoid touching the stem with your fingers and thumbs, as it is very easy to damage the delicate tissues. Remove the bottom set of leaves and immediately place the cutting into the rooting medium. Add a label with the cultivar name and the date, water with a fine spray and place in a propagator. You may use rooting powder, but it is not really necessary. Keep the propagator with a bottom temperature of 15.5–21°C (60–70°F), in good light, but not in direct sunlight, and the cuttings will root in 14–28 days. When rooted the cuttings take on a fresher, brighter appearance and start to make new tip growth. At this point, gradually increase the ventilation in the propagator to acclimatize the cuttings to the drier outside air and harden them off.

SEMI-RIPE CUTTINGS

In the summer, most plants are flowering and the stems have started to ripen. If you wish to take cuttings in this period, take a longer cutting with a heel, up to five pairs of leaves and the growing tip. Remove all flower buds, treat the bottom node and stem with fresh rooting powder or gel, and then treat as soft cuttings.

TYPES OF CUTTING

A semi-ripe cutting (left), consisting of a side shoot removed with a strip of bark from the parent stem, is similar to a hardwood cutting. On the right is a long semi-ripe cutting split into different types of cutting that could be used if propagation material is limited for an individual cultivar.

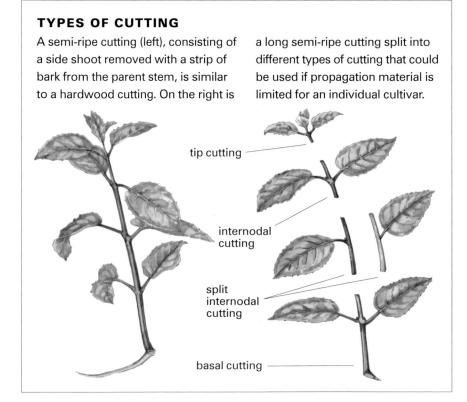

tip cutting

internodal cutting

split internodal cutting

basal cutting

HARDWOOD CUTTINGS

In the late summer and autumn, when the wood is ripe, it is possible to take hardwood cuttings with a heel. To do this it is necessary to tear off a whole side shoot with a heel of bark from the parent stem. Remove any flowers or buds, and treat similarly to soft cuttings. This type of cutting will also often root if inserted into sandy soil in a shady spot outside.

CUTTING COMPOST

Use commercial cutting compost (soil mix), or even better, try two parts of sifted moss peat mixed with one part of washed sharp sand or 2–3mm (½–⅛in) grit and one part of vermiculite or perlite. This gives an open, free-draining mixture with few nutrients which will encourage rapid root formation.

PROPAGATORS

Commercial nurseries use heated propagating benches with overhead misting, and often root directly into sand. Amateur growers can rarely invest in anything quite as elaborate, but there are a number of other solutions:

- electrically heated, gravel tray-sized propagators with vented plastic lids
- similar unheated ones, placed over a greenhouse heater
- plastic covers that fit on to seed trays or pots
- cut-off plastic bottles, or plastic bags fixed above pots with rubber bands

taking cuttings

1 Using a sharp knife, remove a suitable cutting from its parent plant.

2 Prepare cutting medium, using two parts of sifted peat, one part of horticultural grit or coarse sand and one part of vermiculite or perlite.

3 Fill a cell strip with cutting medium. Remove the lower leaves from the stem and insert into a prepared hole in the cutting medium. Add a cultivar label to each cell.

4 Moisten the prepared cell strip filled with cuttings with an overhead spray of water, before placing in the propagator.

CONTAINERS

There are many choices for cutting containers, including seed trays, plug trays and small shallow pots. Trays with individual compartments are an excellent choice. The trays with 60 small cells that fit into a standard seed tray, and split into strips of 12, are very good. They keep each cutting separate, with its own label, prevent the roots intermingling, and make it easier to pot up the cuttings later. A single cell is easily cut out to give away.

Below left The above late summer cuttings well-rooted eight weeks later. Spring cuttings would root in five to six weeks.

Below Some commercial and home-recycled propagators for fuchsias.

potting on and multi-planting

As with most pot plants, fuchsias grown in pots need to be moved to progressively larger pots as they grow. If allowed to become pot-bound in their final pot, they will need extra frequent watering and feeding, but will probably flower profusely – the plant's way of ensuring reproduction when it feels its survival is under threat.

1 Carefully remove a rooted cutting from its rooting cell.

2 Add compost (soil mix) into the bottom of a clean 6cm (2½in) pot, adjusting the amount to ensure the cutting is at the same level as in the rooting cell.

3 Add compost to fill the rest of the air space in the pot, tapping it on a solid surface to make the contents settle.

4 Water in the cutting with an overhead spray and place the pot in a warm position, out of draughts and scorching direct sun.

1 Add compost so that the smaller pot sits inside, level with the rim. Fill the gap between the pots with compost. Carefully remove the inner pot, taking care not to disturb the contents.

2 Remove the plant to be potted on from its smaller pot. Drop the plant into the prepared moulded compost in the larger pot.

3 Tap the pot to settle the plant and top up with more compost. Keep the plant moist by using an overhead spray.

potting up to a 6cm (2½in) pot

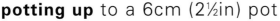

potting on to a 7.5cm (3in) pot

It is important to increase the pot size gradually, rather than moving a plant straight from a small pot to a much larger one. There are two reasons for this. Firstly, it is very difficult to water the pot correctly, since a lot of the compost (soil mix) will stay wet, then it will start to go stale and the roots will avoid it. Secondly, if you do manage to water correctly, the roots will tend to go straight down through the compost to the bottom of the pot, and then start to coil around, but the bulk of the compost will be unused until the formation of branching roots. To keep the compost and roots healthy, it is important to have a cycle of being wetted, drying out and then being rewetted. This cycle sucks in air to the compost every time the pot dries out, which is important for the health of both the roots and the compost. The gradual increase in pot size will mean that the compost is more evenly filled with roots, so the water is used more quickly, thus keeping the cycle going, and also allowing the plant to make the best use of the limited space.

POTTING ON SINGLE PLANTS

A suggested sequence is as follows: pot up a rooted cutting, starting with a 6cm (2½in) pot, then move it to a 7.5cm (3in) pot, then 9cm (3½in), 11cm (4¼in), 13cm (5in) and finally a 15cm (6in) pot. This sequence will give approximately the same percentage increase in compost volume at each potting-on stage. It is not necessary to use the actual pot sizes listed, but the principle is important. If you wish to go beyond a 15cm (6in) pot, you can continue to an 18cm (7in) pot and onwards in 5cm (2in) steps. If plants are growing very strongly, then it may be possible to miss out one pot size in the sequence, but water it very sparsely for the next two weeks, forcing roots to search out the new compost.

POTTING ON TO LARGE CONTAINERS

Take similar care when planting up a large pot with fuchsias alone, or fuchsias with other container plants. Often, in this situation, you might use a few plants from 13cm (5in) pots and the rest from 9cm (3½in) pots. This will lead to a similar situation to the over-potting described earlier, and watering should be carried out with great care. After planting, water sufficiently to settle the plants in, but not so much as to soak the compost completely. Then keep the pot as dry as possible for a period of three to four weeks in early spring, or two to three weeks in late spring, to encourage the roots to penetrate right through the pot. When the roots are short of water they will spread out and go looking for it. After this period, increase the watering and treat the plants as normal.

POTTING UP MULTI-PLANTS

The well-known technique of multi-planting is used for growing "pot mum" chrysanthemums by commercial growers, and this technique is also applicable to fuchsias if you would like to grow a large pot plant quickly. There are three different ways of doing this. The first and most tricky method is to root many cuttings together in a single pot,

growing multi-plants from tip cuttings

1 Choose a donor plant with plenty of cutting material. Take cuttings in the normal way.

2 Place one cutting in the centre of a 9cm (3½in) pot, and another six in a ring around the outside.

3 Add a label, water in and place in a propagator, or add a transparent pot cover to the pot.

growing multi-plants from rooted cuttings

1 Place a rooted cutting into the centre of a 9cm (3½in) pot, with the soil level just below the rim.

2 Add another four or five cuttings of the same cultivar equally spaced around the pot edge.

3 Add compost (soil mix), filling the gaps between the cuttings. Tap to settle the pot, and water them in.

shown in the sequence above (growing multi-plants from tip cuttings). This method needs great care to prevent botrytis when growing on because of the crowding of green stems and leaves.

The second method is to use separately rooted cuttings and pot several of them together in a single pot, shown in the sequence above (growing multi-plants from rooted cuttings).

The final method is to take larger plants growing in 7.5cm (3in) or 9cm (3½in) pots and put five or more of them into a larger 20cm (8in) pot. This method is much easier for those who do not have good propagating facilities. You can use purchased plants from a nursery and plant them up in the spring when the main frost danger has passed. Care needs to be taken with watering until the plants are established. Refer to the instructions for potting on to large containers (above).

Left A small flowering plant of the Triphylla cultivar 'Thalia' in a terracotta (clay) pot against a background of old clay pots.

training shrub and bush fuchsias

Most fuchsias seen growing in gardens, whether in large containers or planted in the ground, are growing as shrubs, since this is their natural form. The graceful, arching growths of the *F. magellanica* variants, gently swaying with their flowers in the summer breeze, are a beautiful example of this style of growth.

When a fuchsia is grown from a cutting without being stopped, the natural form is rather like a Christmas tree, although this depends on how naturally self-branching and upright the cultivar is. When the centre growth is cut, or otherwise broken or killed by frost, the new shoots grow up from the base to create the shrub shape. We need to help nature to create the desired shape right from the beginning. This intervention can be only two or three steps to make a fuchsia shrub for the garden, or up to ten steps or more to grow a large specimen plant for a pot or an exhibition.

There is one main difference between shrub and bush training: a shrub consists of a central growth and shoots which grow up from underneath the soil around the centre, while a bush is grown on a short single stem growing up from the ground.

SHRUB AND BUSH STRUCTURES

In a shrub structure (left), a number of main stems grow from the ground, self-branching above to form the structure. A bush structure (right) is grown from a single central stem growing from the ground with side branches forming the structure.

SHRUB TRAINING

Start with a rooted cutting. If you have taken this yourself, use one that you originally cut just below a node, since this will encourage growths from below the surface. Pot the cutting into a 6cm (2½in) pot and stop the cutting by removing the growing tip once it has grown to three pairs of leaves. This will

stopping to create a shrub

1 Pot up a selected fuchsia cutting into a 6cm (2½in) pot and grow it on until it has four pairs of leaves and a distinct growing tip.

2 Remove the growing tip and allow the side shoots to develop. Later on, the lowest shoots will be below the soil level.

stopping to create a bush

1 Pot up a selected fuchsia cutting into a 6cm (2½in) pot and grow it on until it has five pairs of leaves and a distinct growing tip.

2 Remove the growing tip and then remove the bottom two pairs of leaves and side shoots to leave a clear, short stem.

encourage the formation of side shoots. Check the growth of the roots and when the main roots start to curl around the bottom of the pot, move it on to a 7.5cm (3in) pot, lowering the plant slightly in the pot, and water in gently. Give the plant a 90-degree turn every two to three days, or more frequently if you are growing it on a windowsill.

When the resultant side shoots have grown to two pairs of leaves, stop them by pinching out the growing tips again. You often find that certain cultivars will grow additional side shoots between the junction of the first side shoot and the main stem, especially at the point of removal of the main growing tip. This is a bonus, so just treat them in the same way as the other side shoots and they will add to the density and number of flowers.

This method will be ideal for the basic training of a shrub for use in the garden. You should continue to pot it on as it grows, before hardening it off to plant outside. If you wish, continue to stop every one or two pairs of leaves to create a specimen plant, but remember that every stop made delays flowering by approximately three weeks.

BUSH TRAINING

A fuchsia bush grows on a single stem, which for exhibition purposes should not exceed 4cm (1½in). For garden use, this may be longer, but still not more than 7.5cm (3in). Take a fuchsia cutting and remove the lowest side shoots and leaves so that the cutting has a clear stem of 4cm (1½in) showing above the compost (soil mix) and three pairs of leaves. Place the cutting in a 6cm (2½in) pot and stop the growth by removing the growing tip. When the side shoots have started to form, stop the bottom two sets at two pairs of leaves and the upper set at one pair of leaves. Grow on as for shrub training above.

When the resultant side shoots have grown to one pair of leaves, stop them by pinching out the growing tips again. Treat all the side shoots in the same way and continue the process until the plant is in a 13cm (5in) pot, lowering the plant slightly if the basal stem has grown too long.

Right This large tub planted with a shrub fuchsia, placed as a central feature in a lawn, contrasts nicely with the wall and fence behind it.

potting on a shrub in clay pots

1 Because clay pots are much thicker than plastic pots, the moulding technique shown earlier cannot be used. The cultivar shown here is 'London 2000', ready to be moved from a 7.5cm (3in) pot to a 10cm (4in) pot.

2 Add a few pieces of broken clay pot over the drainage hole to ensure it is not blocked, and to keep the new compost (soil mix) in the pot.

3 Add soil-based compost to the pot, covering the broken pot at the base, so that the plant will sit at the same level or slightly lower than before.

4 Place the plant in the pot and add more compost around the sides, filling all air voids and tapping the pot to settle the contents.

5 Press the compost down gently, but take care not to compact it too much. Finally, water the plant in sparingly.

growing a standard fuchsia

A fuchsia grown as a standard is an excellent way to display the spectacular beauty of the fuchsia flower. To be in proportion, the head of a mature flowering standard fuchsia should be approximately one-third of the overall height, and if grown in a pot, a 1.8m (6ft) full standard needs one that is 30cm (12in) across.

A standard fuchsia is the easiest trained form to grow. Choose a suitable vigorous, upright cultivar such as 'Checkerboard', 'Display' or 'Snowcap', and follow the instructions below.

Below right A first-year full standard fuchsia 'Snowcap' placed on a lawn in a 20cm (8in) pot. The red and white flowers stand out beautifully against the green foliage and against the large *Fatsia japonica* visible in the background.

STARTING THE PROCESS
Start as early in the season as possible, or grow from a late summer/autumn cutting over the winter indoors on a windowsill, in a heated greenhouse, or in a conservatory. Either take a cutting yourself, or buy a suitable young plant from a nursery. Make sure it is unstopped, with the growing tip intact, and look for leaves in sets of three instead of pairs as this type gives an extra branch in each set in the head, allowing it to fill more quickly.

GROWING THE WHIP (STEM)
Pot the cutting up into a 6–7.5cm (2½–3in) pot and, looking down from above, insert a split cane as close to the main stem as possible between the leaves. Make sure the cane is straight. As the plant begins to grow, start to remove the lowest side shoots, leaving the top three sets and the growing tip in place. These young shoots are very easy to snap out, but do not remove the main leaves on the stem. Turn the plant one-quarter of a turn every two days (every day on a windowsill) to keep it growing evenly. As the stem starts to develop, fix it regularly to the cane using suitable ties. Check the ties regularly, because they will quickly cut into the soft stem if they are too tight.

STANDARD STRUCTURE
The stages of growing a standard fuchsia (from left to right). The first picture shows growing the stem – notice the leaves and top side shoots left on the plant. In the centre, the standard has nearly reached the desired height and removal of the main growing tip is imminent. The last picture shows the dormant structure of the finished standard without leaves.

changing a standard cane

1

2

3

4

1 Training of the head of this half standard has started, but the old cane is not long enough.

2 Remove the ties carefully from the stem and cane. Remove the existing cane while supporting the stem.

3 Insert a longer cane and replace the ties, ensuring the stem is straight against the cane. Pay attention to the ties supporting the developing head.

4 The standard now has a new cane that is long enough for the final plant.

As soon as the roots have reached the bottom of the pot and started to coil around, pot on to the next pot size. Make sure you loosen the ties and push the cane to the bottom of the new pot before re-tightening them. It is essential not to let the roots become pot-bound while growing the stem as this often initiates flower buds, which means the plant will not produce the side shoots needed to make the head. Feed regularly with a quarter-strength high-nitrogen feed, and mist the plant frequently. If you wish to avoid this stem growing stage, you can buy a whip directly from a specialist nursery.

FORMING THE HEAD

When the stem (whip) has reached the desired height, take out the growing tip, leaving sufficient side shoots to make the head. A guide is 2–3 sets for a mini standard, 3 sets for a quarter standard, 3–4 sets for a half standard and 4 sets for a full standard, but it will depend on the cultivar, and also on the stem length between the leaves. Pinch out the side shoots on the lower sets at two pairs of leaves and on the upper set at one pair of leaves. Often, additional side shoots will form at each break, especially with the top set, and these are treated in the same way. Stop all resulting side shoots once again at one pair of leaves, and then once more. Gradually remove the leaves from the stem and tie the standard stem in well, especially within the head itself, to prevent the risk of the whole head being snapped off by the wind.

ALLOWING THE STANDARD TO FLOWER

For the final tying of the stem, PVC adhesive insulating tape is excellent, since it stretches and is waterproof. The young standard will benefit from a spell outside to strengthen it up and form the wood necessary in the main structure. Do not pot it on again at this stage, as being root-bound helps to give more flowers. It is important to ensure any young standards are well supported to prevent them being blown over and damaged.

Below The head of a miniature standard grown from the cultivar 'Midwinter'. This is a beautiful cultivar with single white flowers and small mid-green, slightly matt foliage.

growing pillars and pyramids

If you want a different challenge in fuchsia training, try growing a pyramid or a pillar. These can grow to more than 3m (10ft) tall and can be a very impressive sight. It is possible to grow a small one in a single season if you choose a fast-growing variety, but a large specimen will take three years or more.

Right A hardy fuchsia clambering up a brick wall surrounded by other plants in a well-protected garden. In this kind of sheltered environment, some fuchsias make excellent climbing plants.

Before embarking on this challenge, make sure you have enough space in a heated greenhouse to keep the plant over the winter, unless you use a hardy variety.

PILLAR TECHNIQUE

The first thing to consider is how the plant should look when the pillar is completed. The aim is to make a graceful column with proportions of about 4:1 height to diameter, covered in flower. The easiest way to do this is to use the twin stem approach, described below, which will allow your pillar to grow up to 1.5m (5ft) in one season.

Take a cutting of a vigorous self-branching cultivar and grow it up to three pairs of leaves before removing the growing tip. Allow two laterals from just below the stop to form, and remove all others. Then start to train the laterals upward, supported by two canes close together or one cane with longer ties. Decide on the final height of the

PILLAR STRUCTURE

This twin-stem pillar has been grown on two growths from a single central stem, one trained as a tall narrow bush and the other as a stretched standard to form a single structure.

growing a pillar

1 Pot up a fuchsia cutting into a 6cm (2½in) pot and grow on until it has three pairs of leaves and a growing tip. A vigorous growing culitvar is needed for this; the variety used here is 'Katie Susan'.

2 The growing tip is removed to leave two or three pairs of leaves, depending on how long you wish the main stem to be. After the stop allow only the two side shoots from the top of the plant to grow on.

PYRAMID STRUCTURE

When training a fuchsia pyramid, the alternate stopping of the leader and the branches creates the desired shape. Continue the process until you attain the desired height for the specimen.

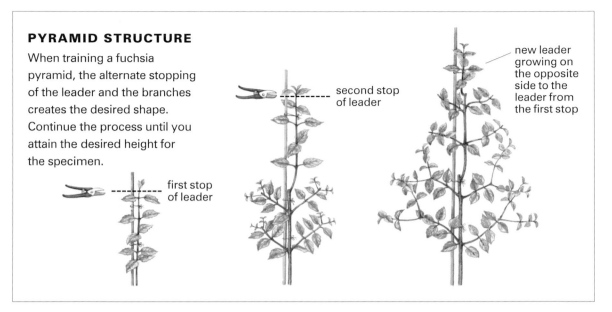

first stop of leader

second stop of leader

new leader growing on the opposite side to the leader from the first stop

pillar, and grow one stem like a stretched bush to half this height, and the other like a standard to the full height. For the stretched bush side, leave all the lateral growths and stop them at one or two pairs of leaves, and for the standard side, remove all the lateral growths except the top three or four sets. Pot on as soon as the roots start to curl round the pot. As early as you can, put in the final cane, as replacing the ties becomes more difficult later.

When the bush side reaches half the final desired height, remove the growing tip and continue to stop at one or two pairs of leaves. When the standard stem reaches half the desired height, allow the laterals to stay on and pinch them at one or two pairs of leaves. From now on, stop the shoots at alternately one or two sets of leaves to maintain the shape.

When the standard stem reaches the desired height, pinch out the growing tip, and also pinch out the laterals to complete the desired shape. Finally, once you are happy with the overall shape of the plant, stop pinching the shoots and allow them to flower.

PYRAMID TECHNIQUE

When fully grown, this should look like a Christmas tree, with approximate proportions of 6:4 height to diameter at the base, the diameter decreasing steadily toward the top to form a pyramid or cone shape. A pyramid is best grown as a single plant, and it can take two or three years to grow.

Take a cutting of a vigorous growing cultivar with strong, stiff lateral growths. Grow it upward to a height of 25cm (10in) with a cane to support it, and then remove the growing tip. This stop will result in a surge of growth to the laterals, which is important for the shape. Remove the lowest pair of laterals to give a short single stem at the base. When the two new shoots start to develop, decide which is the stronger growing one and remove the other. Now you will be growing the stronger shoot on up as the new leader. When it has grown 7–10 cm (3–4in), stop all the laterals on the first part of the stem. The leader will get a new surge of growth. When it has grown the same number of joints as the first part of the stem, pinch out the growing tip again. This time remove the opposite shoot to the first stem stop, so the growth goes in the opposite direction.

Continue growing in this way, potting on, changing the support cane, adjusting ties and feeding with high-nitrogen fertilizer, alternately stopping the leader and the laterals to form the desired shape. If the laterals are growing too weakly on one side of the plant, simply lay the plant down horizontally with the weak leaders positioned vertically for a few days, and the resultant change in the flow of sap will boost the growth. Note that you will need to create special supports or hangers to do this. Grow on until the desired height is reached, then allow the pyramid to flower. Trim it back to retain the shape in the late summer or early autumn, and keep the plant ticking over in green leaf through the winter.

Above left A plant of the cultivar 'Midwinter' is suitable for growing as a pyramid.

Below A narrow pyramid of the cultivar 'Brutus', approximately 2.1m (7ft) tall, tied to an old pear tree.

training other fuchsia shapes

There are many different trained shapes for fuchsias, which will give interesting results. Below are brief descriptions of a few, ranging from novelty shapes, which are a form of topiary, through small dwarfed bonsai forms, to large structures such as fans and espaliers that are big enough to cover a good-sized wall.

Above A novelty hen shape created by growing the fuchsia 'Lottie Hobby' and variegated thyme around a wire former, bedding in moss and potting compost (soil mix).

Right 'Lottie Hobby' is an Encliandra hybrid with quite strong and vigorous wiry growth, with small leaves and small red flowers. It is an excellent cultivar for creating topiary shapes around wire formers.

Far right A superb bonsai grown from *F. magellanica* var. *molinae*. This hardy species variant can grow more than 1.5m (5ft) in a season planted in the ground, but in this case has miniaturized growth.

The training of several fuchsia shapes is described here, apart from the espalier, which is trained in a similar way to fruit trees such as a conservatory peach tree.

NOVELTY SHAPES

Commercial wire formers are available in a variety of shapes for this type of plant training, but if you are feeling adventurous, why not make one yourself? A spiral is the easiest shape to make, or you could try the number of your house as something rather different. The best cultivars to use are from the Encliandra group, for example 'Lottie Hobbie', *F. microphylla* subsp. *hemsleyana*, *F. microphylla* subsp. *hidalgensis* or *F.* x *bacillaris*. These fuchsias have very small foliage, but will grow quickly enough to cover the structure in a season.

Place the chosen wire former in a suitable pot filled with compost (soil mix) and planted with up to five plants of your desired cultivar, depending on the size and shape of the wire former. These plants should have been stopped twice. Secure them with wire hoops or a cane if necessary. Grow them on, keeping the pot on the dry side to encourage rapid

rooting through the pot. When the growths reach the edge of the wire former, start to train and twist them along the wire, stopping any growths that want to continue growing straight outward. Direct the growths to fill the whole surface of the shape, stopping them if necessary to increase the number of side growths to fill a space, then keep the plants clipped to maintain the shape.

BONSAI FUCHSIAS

Fuchsias can be grown as bonsai specimens, but this is a long-term project. When growing fuchsias this way, dwarfing of the leaves occurs, but the flowers will stay at the normal size for the cultivar, and therefore it is best to choose a small single-flowered fuchsia. To start with, you need

planting a bonsai

1 Dig up a dormant woody plant of a hardy fuchsia as a basis for a bonsai. Prune the roots so that it will fit into a shallow bonsai container. The cultivar used here is 'Genii'.

2 Prune the top growth back to a number of short growths and remove any old foliage. Further hard pruning of the main stem will be needed when growth starts to create the bonsai growth habit.

3 Pot up in a gritty compost (soil mix), blended to contain a lower level of nutrients than usual. This prevents any rapid growth.

4 Gently water to settle into the container. Allow the plant to settle down for a few weeks, then start misting the wood to encourage it into growth.

an older plant that has formed a good woody structure, or a plant grown deliberately as a bonsai. To prepare it for transfer to a bonsai container, pot it back to ever smaller pot sizes over six months, step by step. This will involve some root pruning of the tap and major roots and reducing the top growth by approximately 40 per cent, removing any unwanted laterals and leaves.

Shape the branches gently to the desired position with wire, and gradually expose the top of the uppermost roots. When the plant is ready, move it to a bonsai container, using a compost containing some grit and charcoal. Prune the roots further as necessary and run the uppermost roots over a suitable smooth stone. Grow the plant outside, protected from hot sun. Feed it with a balanced fertilizer, keeping it moist but not saturated, and continue to shape the plant by removing large leaves and strong growths.

FAN SHAPES

A fan needs a lot of support to keep it in shape, so it must grow against a wall or fence where it can be tied in securely. You can choose to grow a small fan if you do not have much space, but if you continue to grow a specimen year on year it will become quite large. It is the most labour-intensive structure to grow because of the amount of tying in required.

You can grow a fan from either a single plant or three plants of the same cultivar. It is essential to have all of the main growths and stems growing in the same plane, so it is best to pick a cutting of a strong-growing but slightly lax cultivar such as 'Waveney Gem'. Stop the cutting when it has made four pairs of leaves and remove the first and third

sets of side shoots, so that all the side shoots are growing in the same plane.

Pot on as soon as roots start to coil around the bottom of the pot, and start to make the support structure with canes. Insert five canes in a fan shape with the central one vertical, and tie in two horizontal ones to make the framework rigid. Grow up the laterals to cover the framework, tying them in as necessary and stopping them periodically to increase the number of leaders to cover the structure. Pull the side shoots from the leaders through to the front, tie them in and stop them. When the main leaders are close to the edge of the frame, stop them all again and allow the fan to flower.

FAN STRUCTURE

When beginning a fan (left), the main shoots of the starting growth should be in the same plane.

Later (right), the fan growths have been stopped and the side shoots cover more of the frame.

planting in containers

Many gardens now have extensive patios, terraces and other paved or gravelled areas, and of course many have no exposed soil at all. With an imaginative choice of containers, and a careful selection of fuchsias and other plants, you can create all kinds of different moods, ambiances and garden styles in these areas.

A tremendous variety of different containers are available from nurseries, garden centres, DIY superstores and specialist potteries in many materials and colours. When choosing a container, remember that fuchsias like to keep their roots cool. Porous terracotta (clay) pots are the perfect choice, as the evaporation cools them down and they also help keep the compost (soil mix) aerated.

FUCHSIA REQUIREMENTS

The most important requirement for fuchsias is good drainage, because although they love moisture, they detest waterlogging of the growing medium. Therefore, it is vital to ensure that good drainage holes are provided and to increase the number or size of the holes if they are not good enough for the purpose.

Right An informal arrangement of terracotta (clay) urn pots piled on stones with flowering fuchsia plants growing among them.

planting a large pot

1 Assemble all the plants you wish to use. Add broken pots or polystyrene (Styrofoam) as crocking.

2 Part-fill the pot with potting compost (soil mix). Arrange the plants in the pot. Lift out the plants and replace each with an empty pot of the same size.

3 Add potting compost, working it around the edges of the empty pots. Lift out an empty pot and drop in the plant. Repeat for the other plants.

4 Top up with potting compost and settle the contents. Water sparingly and grow on.

To protect the pot's drainage, especially in large containers where a soil-based compost is used, it is important to add drainage material to the bottom of the container to ensure the holes stay open. An ideal way is to place curved pieces of broken clay pots over the holes, followed by a layer of stones of various sizes, broken expanded polystyrene (Styrofoam) or similar materials. When you add the compost on top of these pieces, they will stop most of it reaching the bottom of the pot and potentially blocking the drainage holes. To further improve drainage, you can stand large clay or stone pots on special feet which raise the pot approximately 2½cm (1in) off the ground.

PLANTING LARGE CONTAINERS

The best time to plant up large containers with fuchsias is in the spring, when the plants are growing strongly and the roots will rapidly expand

and penetrate the compost. A good range of plants is available in the spring, since the garden centres and nurseries expect and prepare for the demand. Plan in advance the plants you would like to use and either grow them yourself or purchase them. The actual week of planting will depend on your local climate and what extra protection, such as a greenhouse, you have available to protect from them late frosts.

You can apply the planting technique described in the pictorial sequences for the planting of any large container. Additionally, this technique may be used for any type of plant that is grown or purchased in a smaller pot when you transfer it to a larger one, as it minimizes the damage to the plants and makes it easier to fill all of the spaces with compost, not leaving any empty spaces. You can choose to add slow-release fertilizer to the compost or feed regularly with soluble fertilizers, but be careful to do either one or the other, or you may risk over-feeding or starving the plants. There is sufficient fertilizer in the new compost to last for about four to six weeks after planting, so do not start using liquid feeds before this time has elapsed.

It is also very important to control the watering for the first weeks, keeping the containers rather dry until plants have become established and made good root growth through the container. Therefore, if you are growing newly planted containers outside, take the precaution of keeping them under cover when heavy rain is likely, to prevent them becoming too wet, as this will slow down the growth.

planting a chimney pot

1 Use a "bishop" type of chimney pot as an ideal planter. Cut a piece of heavy wire mesh so that it fits inside the cowl and sits on the chimney body. Place finer mesh on top of the heavy mesh.

2 Add a layer of coarse stone chippings to act as a bed for the potting compost (soil mix).

3 Add a layer of potting compost. Choose the plants and find empty plastic pots of the same size that they are in.

4 Set the empty pots into the chimney pot, spacing them evenly, and add potting compost until it is full.

5 Knock a small plant out of its pot, then lift its corresponding empty pot out of the chimney pot and drop the plant into the empty hole. Repeat with the other plants.

6 Add more potting compost to fill any depressions and voids. Settle the contents, then water them in sparingly. Grow on in a sheltered position.

Far left This large specimen fuchsia plant is growing in a decorative plastic pot and just coming into flower. Beside it is a variegated ivy.

Left Standing on steps, this large mixed pot is planted with geraniums, busy Lizzie, helichrysum and the fuchsias 'Coralle', 'Seventh Heaven', 'Cambridge Louie' and 'Happy Wedding Day'.

planting as summer bedding

Fuchsias make excellent plants for all kind of borders and beds as temporary summer residents. You can use them within bedding schemes, for edging and even in the rockery. Standard fuchsias and other trained fuchsia shapes are excellent for raising the height in borders, either planted out directly into the soil or sunk in their existing pots.

Fuchsias are easy to grow, reliable and easy to use as summer bedding. There is a tremendous range of different flower and even leaf colours to use. They can used throughout the summer, then either be discarded in the autumn or potted up and overwintered for use the next year, using techniques described later.

Below An unusual summer bedding arrangement of fuchsias in a bed divided into compartments with low hedging. Other large fuchsias are visible in the background, along with *Agaves* in large pots.

SOIL PREPARATION

Fuchsias are quite tolerant of different soil types, but they do not like being waterlogged and they are quite greedy feeders. They will benefit from extra organic matter, such as leaf mould, well-rotted compost (rotten vegetable matter) or any

equivalent materials, which will improve both fertility and texture. If the soil is very heavy, you could also dig in some horticultural grit. The best time to dig over the border is in the winter or early spring, so that you can leave it a while to settle.

TEMPORARY BEDDING

Any fuchsias bedded out in a border as temporary residents should be planted normally, with the plant crown (the soil level in the pot) at ground level. If you are planting out any double-flowering types with heavy blooms where the growths are a little soft or lax, stake and tie the main branches to give some additional support. They still benefit from a

planting fuchsias as edging plants

good addition of organic material in the soil, but
drainage is not as critical in summer as in winter.
Use a good general fertilizer when planting, and
feed again during the summer following the
manufacturer's instructions.

Plant fuchsias with sufficient distance between
the plants for them to fill up the spaces by the
middle of the summer. The actual planting distance
depends on the size of the plant when first planted
out, and the typical growth of the cultivar. As an
example, you might be planting out the Triphylla
cultivar 'Thalia' from 12cm (5in) pots, each plant
having about 20–30cm (8–12in) of growth. They will
need to be spaced with about 30cm (12in) between
the centre of each plant. One of the best ways to
do this if you want blocks of the same cultivar is in
a triangular layout. Plant two cultivars 30cm (12in)
apart, and plant the next one at a point halfway
between and 26cm (10in) behind the first two,
forming an equilateral triangle. Extend this to a
three-by-three triangle with three more plants, then
a four-by-four with four more and so on. Using this
arrangement of plants, you can create different
shapes, ensuring the plants are always the correct
distance apart. Of course, if you prefer a more
natural look, you can just mix and match the
cultivars as you wish.

Small, compact-growing fuchsias are excellent
for use as edging, planted as shown in the step
sequence above. Fuchsias that typically only grow
to 30–45cm (12–18in), such as 'Tom Thumb' and
'Happy', or fuchsias with variegated or light foliage,
such as 'Tom West', 'Abigail Reine' and 'Sunray',
are good choices for edging plants.

PLANTING OUT STANDARDS

Standards are very useful to raise the height of a
planting scheme, but they are tender even when
grown from a hardy cultivar, and need returning
to the greenhouse for frost protection during the
winter. Before planting them out, they need to be
hardened up by standing them outside during the
day for two weeks, then finally overnight as well for
another few days, with support to prevent them
from falling over. They may be planted directly into
the ground or have their pots sunk in the ground
with their rims just above soil level.

The major additional requirement when planting
out standard fuchsias is to ensure proper support
for the head. Tie in the trunk and head well to a
strong cane; some additional support is a good
idea, especially with younger standards that have
not developed heavy wood. When planting close
to a wall or fence, fix some horizontal struts and tie
them to the main cane, or alternatively use a strong
stake behind the plant with similar horizontal struts.

planting a hardy fuchsia bed

Permanent planting of hardy fuchsias in the garden is a wonderful way to get a superb display of flowers from early summer to late autumn, with very little maintenance needed. There is a wide range of hardy fuchsias available, most of which can grow anything from 30cm (18in) up to 1.6m (5ft) in one season. There is also a good range of colours.

When you are planning to create a hardy fuchsia bed, a certain amount of preparation is advisable; as usual in gardening, careful planning in advance will give better and more long-lasting results.

THE SITE
It is important to look hard at the area you are going to use for planting your hardy fuchsias.
- Good drainage should be at the top of your list. Waterlogged soil in the winter will kill the fuchsias, so avoid low-lying areas likely to flood. Heavy soils need improvement with organic matter and anything else to improve drainage, such as grit or sand.
- Wind exposure, especially in an area with very cold winter temperatures, will mean you can only use the hardiest cultivars.
- Sunshine is not such a problem. Fuchsias planted in the ground will tolerate the sun quite well as long as they are kept watered in long dry spells, but if you can provided some shade from the midday and early afternoon sun that will help avoid stress on hot days.

SOIL PREPARATION
The area you have chosen to plant your hardy bed needs preparation. The preparation depends on the soil type: sandy soils need extra organic material, and heavy clay types need both organic material and coarse sand and grit to improve drainage. Dig it over, and remove any perennial weeds and roots. This should ideally be done in the autumn so that the area can settle and weather in the winter.

Left An established bed full of hardy fuchsias, their stems entwining and reaching heights of more than 2m (6ft).

PLANNING

Read the directory in this and other books, and obtain catalogues from different nurseries. In these, you will find descriptions and illustrations of different hardy fuchsias, with their flowers and colours, their growth habits and the heights to which they will grow in a typical season. Note that these are average measurements, and are based on areas where winter frosts will cut them down to the ground. If you are lucky enough to live in a milder area, they will continue to grow from toward the top of the previous year's growth and will reach greater heights each year.

Make a list of the cultivars you want, and plan how to plant them, thinking about the heights, colours and any other types of plants you will interplant. Generally, the larger plants should be at the back and the smaller ones at the front.

OBTAINING PLANTS

If you have a greenhouse, you can probably get some cuttings of hardy fuchsias from friends and neighbours and grow them on over the winter. If you wish to order from a nursery, do so in good time, as ideally you should have well-developed plants in 13–15cm (5–6in) pots by planting-out time

planting a hardy fuchsia

1 Scoop a shallow depression out of the soil approximately 65cm (26in) wide and 10cm (4in) deep at the centre.

2 Dig a hole large enough at the centre to take the root ball of the plant, adding some general fertilizer at the bottom.

3 Place the hardy fuchsia plant in the hole so that the surface of the soil around the plant is level with the base of the depression.

4 Firm the soil, then, as the plant grows through the summer, gradually pull back the soil around the plant to fill the depression.

in the late spring or early summer. Place the plants outside on suitable days in mid-spring to harden them off, and finally leave them outside in their pots for a few days before planting out.

PLANTING

First place the plants you are going to use, still in their pots, in their final positions on the bed to get the spacing correct. Mark the positions with canes and remove the plants. For each position, scoop out a shallow depression over a diameter of four to five times the pot diameter and to a depth of 7.5–10cm (3–4in) at the centre. Then make a hole at the centre of the depression slightly larger than the pot, dig in some fertilizer and plant the fuchsia. The soil surface around the plant should be at the level of the bottom of the depression. Firm the soil and water the plant in well. The crown of the plant is now 7.5–10cm (3–4in) lower than the general soil level in the bed. Repeat this procedure for all the other plantings.

As the fuchsias grow and establish through the summer, gradually pull the soil back to its original level, so that the plant crown is covered by 7.5–10cm (3–4in) of soil, watering in dry periods. This added protection of the crown is essential for winter survival, and the first year is the most critical. If it survives, it will probably last for many years.

Below left Growing in front of the *Canna* 'Tchad' is *F. magellanica* var. *riccartonii*, a hardy fuchsia, strong growing and often found naturalized in hedgerows.

Below A hardy fuchsia bed contrasting with the stems of *Verbena bonariensis* in the background.

planting a fuchsia hedge

In milder areas, it is possible to grow hardy fuchsias as exotic and eye-catching hedges. Hedges of *F. magellanica* var. *riccartonii* are a beautiful sight. In gardens, these make a good dividing hedge or an attractive low hedge grown against a fence. It is not a good idea to use fuchsias as boundary hedges except in very mild areas.

Grow fuchsia hedges only in areas of the garden where the average winter conditions will not kill the wood down to the ground, so that you can easily maintain the structure of the hedge. As the hedge grows, its thickness will give the internal growth some extra protection. Even if an extreme winter kills the growth down to the ground, it is possible to re-grow the structure from the basal growths of a hardy fuchsia.

Grow the hedge from a row of plants of the same variety, as different plants develop at different rates and it would be difficult to keep them all in shape as a hedge. Since the hedge will be in flower from midsummer until the end of the autumn, opportunities to clip and shape the hedge are quite limited unless you are willing to sacrifice some flowers.

PREPARATION

Plant fuchsia hedges in a shallow trench to give the maximum protection to the crowns of the plants. You will be expecting your hedge to last for some years, so good preparation of the ground is important. Try to avoid any areas that are prone to waterlogging in the winter, or provide some additional drainage. Dig the ground first, incorporating plenty of organic material to improve and open up the soil structure.

Below A vigorous hardy fuchsia growing more than 2.5m (8ft) tall alongside a brick wall and over a doorway in a garden in the south-west of England. This demonstrates how high a fuchsia hedge can grow in the right conditions.

Finish the preparation by making a shallow trench 15cm (6in) deep, and 45cm (18in) wider than the desired width of the hedge.

PLANTING

Decide how tall and wide you wish the hedge to be, and select a suitable variety. If you want extra thickness, you can plant in a double staggered row. The plants should be spaced about 45cm (18in) apart, unless you are making a low hedge with dwarf cultivars, when a spacing of 30cm (12in) is more appropriate. Estimate how many plants you will need and add a further 10 per cent as a safety margin.

The plants need to be healthy, growing well in 13cm (5in) pots, hardened off and ready for planting in the late spring. If you cannot grow these plants yourself, order them in good time from a reputable fuchsia nursery, making it clear that you are going to use them for a hedge. They will be glad to give you advice on suitable cultivars. Plant the ready plants into the trench in a row, or a staggered double row, making sure that the top of the compost (soil mix) in the pot comes level with the base of the trench. Dress the row with a suitable balanced fertilizer and water the plants in well.

GROWING ON

Grow the plants on with the absolute minimum of pruning, just trimming any wayward branches and enjoying the flowering. Water the hedge well in any dry periods and give it an occasional foliar feed to boost the growth. Gradually pull the earth back into the trench so that the crowns of the plants are 15cm (6in) below soil level.

In mid-autumn, when the growth subsides, trim the shape of the hedge by removing any long straggly growth. Protect the plants with a mulch of leaves or other organic material. During the first winter, protect the hedge with fleece in any very cold frosty periods. Next spring, when new growths have started to appear, remove any dead branches, and give the live growth another trim to get the desired shape. Have a few spare plants ready to replace any which have succumbed to the first winter.

Right This fuchsia is showing its endeavour by growing through and alongside a *Leylandii* hedge. The flowers contrast beautifully with the yellow-green of the *Leylandii*.

planting a hedge

1 When planting a hedge alongside a fence, set out the plants on the prepared soil, staggering them 30cm (12in) apart.

2 Dig a hole in the soil deeper than the depth of the pot. This ensures the crown of the plant will be well below the soil surface.

3 Knock the plant out of its pot, and loosen any long roots. Plant the fuchsia at the bottom of the hole and cover with soil.

4 Water well, and add a mulch of composted bark or similar material to reduce weeds and retain moisture.

DIRECTORY
of fuchsias

More than 10,000 fuchsia cultivars have been introduced since the work of the first fuchsia hybridizers started in the early 19th century. This directory lists over 200 fuchsia cultivars, organized into groups recommended for different purposes, and accompanied by descriptions and many photographs. The descriptions include information about each fuchsia's origin, flower type, size and colour, growth habit and foliage colour, as well as its hardiness and how much sun it will tolerate. For hardy fuchsias that can grow larger from year to year, the average eventual size is also given. This is the perfect resource both for novice growers and keen enthusiasts looking for interesting and unusual varieties.

Left 'Dark Eyes' is a lovely double American cultivar with a deep red tube and sepals and a full violet-blue corolla. It is quite a strong upright bush and makes a good temporary resident in the border.

Above 'Walz Jubelteen' is a lovely single Dutch cultivar with erect pink flowers. It is a strong-growing fuchsia and will make a good standard, a superb garden border plant or a specimen plant.

'Gay Parasol'

'Gay Parasol'

The flowers of this cultivar are well described by its name – they open to a rather flat shape, just like a parasol. They are a medium-sized double with an ivory-green tube, pinkish-white sepals and a burgundy-red, flat rosette-shaped corolla. The plant has strong upright growth with mid-green foliage and makes a very nice half standard, or is equally good as a pot plant. It is one of many excellent introductions by the American hybridist Annabelle Stubbs. Half-hardy; Zones 9–10. Stubbs, USA, 1979.

'Hazel'

This slightly lax cultivar has large double, rather round flowers with a neyron-rose tube, neyron-rose sepals and a corolla of neyron-rose with purple splashed white. The flowers contrast well with the large red-veined lettuce-green foliage and it can be grown up to a weeping full or half standard. It is also useful as a basket plant or a pot plant with support. Half-hardy; Zones 9–10. Richardson, Australia, 1985.

'Joy Patmore'

'Irene van Zoeren'

This bushy cultivar has medium double flowers with a light orange tube, rose-red sepals with yellow-green tips and a lilac-rose corolla with a darker red border to the petals. It has a bushy habit with strongly upright growth and makes a nice quarter or half standard, or a good pot plant or specimen plant. It has mid- to dark green foliage and tolerates full sun. Half-hardy; Zones 9–10. Beije, Netherlands, 1989.

'Jack Acland'

This cultivar has very vigorous stiff trailing growth, with long arched branches and mid-green foliage. It has medium to large single flowers with a medium pink tube, pink slightly recurving sepals and a bell-shaped corolla that opens rose-red and fades to a dark pink. It makes a good weeping half or full standard and is also excellent in a basket. The name is often misspelt as 'Jack Ackland', and it is sometimes confused with the cultivar 'Jack Shaan'. Half-hardy; Zones 9–10. Haag and Son, USA, 1952.

'Joy Patmore'

This striking cultivar has medium single flowers with a white tube, waxy white sepals tipped green and a flared carmine corolla. The colour combination of the flowers is very vivid and they stand out well from the mid-green foliage. It has very strong upright growth and will make an excellent quarter, half or full standard. It will also make a splendid specimen plant, and because of the way it displays its flowers it will also be at home as a summer bedding plant. This cultivar deserves a place in everybody's collection. Half-hardy; Zones 9–10. Turner, UK, 1961.

'Katrina Thompsen'

This exhibition-class cultivar bears small single flowers, but it compensates for that by their sheer number. It has small to medium single flowers with a white-green tube, white sepals and a white corolla. In common with many of the whites, the flower colour will stay white in shade, whereas if it is exposed to more sun it will take on pink hues. It is a vigorous, self-branching and slightly lax bush, and will make a beautiful quarter standard covered in flower that stands out against the small dark green foliage. It is very adaptable and can be grown in other trained forms such as a pyramid or column, or simply used as a pot plant. Its main fault is its susceptibility to fuchsia rust. Half-hardy; Zones 9–10. Wilkinson, UK, 1991.

'Katrina Thompsen'

'Love's Reward'

'Love's Reward'

The name of this cultivar is very apt. It caused a huge stir among fuchsia growers when it was released, with its particularly beautiful flowers. It has small to medium single flowers that are almost semi-erect and held off the mid-green foliage. The flower has a pink tube, pink sepals and a violet-blue corolla with red stamens. The growth is short, bushy and self-branching, and it makes a very striking quarter standard. You will need to remove any dead foliage quickly, since this cultivar is prone to botrytis in the branches caused by rotting leaves. You should also be sparing with watering, as it hates being waterlogged. Half-hardy; Zones 9–10. Bambridge, UK, 1986.

'Lye's Unique'

This is a very old cultivar and perhaps one of the best-known varieties developed by James Lye. The flower is a hanging medium-sized single with a waxy white tube, waxy white sepals and a salmon-orange corolla. The waxy white tube and sepals are a trademark of the Lye varieties. It has upright vigorous growth, with mid-green leaves, and it flowers early and continues blooming throughout the season. It grows easily and quickly to an impressive half or full standard. Half-hardy; Zones 9–10. Lye, UK, 1886.

'Margaret Brown'

This hardy cultivar is one of the best fuchsia varieties. It has small single flowers with a rosy-pink tube and sepals and a light rose bengal corolla with light veining. Its growth is vigorous and upright with light green foliage. It will make a splendid quarter or half standard, or you can grow it as a permanently planted shrub in the garden, where it will give a lot of pleasure for years with its continuous flowering. Hardy; Zones 5–6. Growth 90cm (35in). Awarded an RHS Highly Commended Certificate for hardiness in 1965. Wood, UK, 1939.

'Miss California'

This American introduction has medium to large semi-double flowers with a pink tube, long narrow pink sepals and a flared corolla with white pink-veined petals. It has reasonably vigorous growth with thin wiry stems and a slightly lax habit. The long flowers show up well against the mid-green foliage and it is easy to grow to a quarter or half standard. Half-hardy; Zones 9–10. Hodges, USA, 1950.

'Lye's Unique'

'Margaret Brown'

'Mrs Lovell Swisher'

This is another easy and rewarding fuchsia to grow. The small to medium single flowers have a long pink tube, green and pinkish-white sepals held just above the horizontal, and a deep rose corolla. The growth is vigorous and upright with mid-green leaves. The tremendous number of flowers produced over a long season makes up for their smaller size. It is easy to grow to a quarter, half or full standard, although it is probably at its best as a half. This is another good one for a beginner to try. Half-hardy; Zones 9–10. Evans and Reeves, USA, 1942.

'Nellie Nuttall'

This small showy cultivar is widely used for exhibitions, and when you see it you can understand why. It has small to medium single flowers that are semi-erect and held out from the light mid-green foliage. The tube is small and red, the sepals are crimson and held horizontally and the corolla is white with red veining. The growth is upright and very bushy, and it makes a superb miniature or quarter standard. The growth is probably not vigorous enough to make a large standard unless you have a lot of patience. Try it as an edging plant as well. Hybridized from 'Khada' x 'Icecap'. Half-hardy; Zones 9–10. Roe, UK, 1977.

'Olive Smith'

This cultivar has small single flowers, held semi-erect from the mid-green foliage, with a carmine tube, carmine sepals that curve upward and a crimson corolla. It has vigorous upright self-branching growth, and the sheer number of flowers produced compensates for their small size. It makes a superb quarter, half or full standard and is often seen at exhibitions trained this way. It also makes a good summer bedding plant. Half-hardy; Zones 9–10. Smith, UK, 1991.

'Ortenburger Festival'

This cultivar has a very striking flower that really grabs the attention, especially when it is grown as a standard. It has medium-sized bell-shaped single flowers with a short thick red tube, deep red sepals held just below the horizontal and a violet-blue corolla, which turns reddish on maturity. The growth is upright, bushy and self-branching, and the leaves are dark green and have serrated edges. It makes a very impressive half or full standard, and older specimens have attractive peeling bark. Half-hardy; Zones 9–10. Topperwein, Germany, 1973.

'Olive Smith'

'Paula Jane'

'Paula Jane'

This has medium semi-double flowers with a Venetian pink tube, carmine-rose sepals and a beetroot-purple corolla that matures to ruby red and flares out. The flowers stand out against the shiny light to mid-green foliage. It has a strong upright and bushy growth with very strong stems. It makes an excellent bush and is very amenable to training as a standard. It is at its best as a half standard, but try growing it as a quarter or a full standard as well. It does not have many faults apart from the fact that it does make a lot of pollen, which can be deposited on the leaves, and it also makes seed berries which are very firmly attached and need to be cut off to ensure continued flowering. Half-hardy; Zones 9–10. Tite, UK, 1975.

'Peppermint Stick'

This cultivar has a rather unusual flower, as suggested by its name. It has medium-sized double hanging flowers with a carmine-rose tube, carmine sepals with a white stripe and a corolla with purple centre petals and light carmine outer petals with a purple edge. It is very floriferous for the size of the flower, and the growth is strongly upright with mid-green foliage. The two-tone flowers display well when it is grown as a half standard. It is also a good choice for a pot or bedding plant. Half-hardy; Zones 9–10. Walker and Jones, USA, 1950.

'Royal Velvet'

'Royal Velvet'

This cultivar has medium to large double flowers with a crimson red tube and sepals, and a deep purple corolla splashed with red, which flares very widely open on maturity. The growth is vigorous and upright with bright light to mid-green foliage. It makes an excellent half or even full standard, but it needs pinching well, early in the season. A period grown outside to harden up the growth ensures the branches are strong enough to support the flowers. It really rewards you when you display the flowers at eye level, but also does well as a summer bedder. This is probably one of Waltz's best introductions, though it has some stiff competition. Half-hardy; Zones 9–10. Waltz. USA, 1962.

'Shelford'

This vigorous and very adaptable cultivar has medium-sized single flowers with a baby pink tube, baby pink sepals shading to white and tipped green, and a white corolla. The amount of pink depends on the amount of sun it receives; kept in the shade it is almost white. It is vigorous, self-branching and upright and makes an excellent quarter or half standard with very little effort. The flowers stand out well from the medium-sized mid- to dark green foliage. In all ways this is an excellent cultivar, which can also be used in baskets and as a summer bedding plant. Half-hardy; Zones 9–10. Roe, UK, 1986.

'Sleigh Bells'

This is one of the almost pure white cultivars and has medium-sized single flowers with a white tube, white sepals with green tips and a white corolla. The growth is upright and bushy with mid- to dark green serrated leaves, which contrast beautifully with the flowers. This cultivar has vigorous growth and reaches heights of 2.5m (8ft) in the Californian climate. It makes a very good half standard and is excellent trained as a pyramid or espalier. Half-hardy; Zones 9–10. Schnabel, USA, 1954.

'Sophie Louise'

This is a small-flowered cultivar that always looks most attractive. It has small single flowers, with a greenish-white tube, white sepals and a vivid dark purple corolla, which hold themselves semi-erect, and contrast well with the small mid-green foliage. It has a bushy, self-branching habit and grows quite well, but will not make a big plant quickly. Grow it as a miniature or quarter standard and it will reward you with a tremendous show of flowers. Half-hardy; Zones 9–10. Wilkinson, UK, 1999.

'Sophie Louise'

'Wigan Peer'

'Tom Thumb'

This is a small hardy cultivar, a very old variety which is still widely grown today. Any cultivar that is grown for more than 100 years must surely have some excellent characteristics. It has small single or semi-double flowers with a carmine tube and sepals and a mauve carmine-veined corolla. The flowers hang down among the small, dark green leaves. It has compact upright and bushy growth and makes a superb miniature or quarter standard. It is equally at home in the rockery or used as an edging plant in borders. Hardy; Zone 6. Growth 46cm (18in). Awarded an RHS First Class Certificate for hardiness in 1962. Baudinat, France, 1850.

'Vanessa Jackson'

This cultivar has long, large single flowers with a salmon-red tube, long salmon-orange sepals and a salmon-orange and red corolla with a trumpet shape. The growth is trailing and self-branching with large mid-green leaves. It will make a lovely weeping standard and is also ideal for hanging baskets and pots. Half-hardy; Zones 9–10. Handley, UK, 1980.

'Wigan Peer'

This relatively new cultivar has small to medium compact double flowers with a pink tube, white sepals flushed pale pink and a full white corolla. It is a strong, upright and self-branching cultivar with mid-green foliage, and makes a very good quarter or half standard. It also makes an excellent pot plant. Half-hardy; Zones 9–10. Clark, UK, 1988.

'Winston Churchill'

This lovely free-flowering double-flowered cultivar has medium-sized compact blooms with a pink tube and sepals, and a lavender-blue corolla with reddish veins. It has upright and bushy self-branching growth with wiry stems and rather narrow small mid- to dark green foliage. It makes a very nice quarter or half standard, but also makes a good pot plant. It is a good, reliable cultivar. Half-hardy; Zones 9–10. Garson, USA, 1942.

trained structures

Fuchsia structures such as pyramids and fans are a challenge to grow but very satisfying when they are complete. They are best overwintered in green leaf.

'Amy Lye'

This fuchsia is a cultivar of James Lye, who was one of the earliest producers to grow fuchsia pyramids. This cultivar is free- and early-flowering with medium-sized single flowers, which have a creamy white tube, white sepals tipped green and a coral-orange corolla. The growth is vigorous and spreading with medium-sized dark green leaves and is good for training as any tall growing structure such as a pillar or pyramid. Half-hardy; Zones 9–10. Lye, UK, 1885.

'Brutus'

This is a vigorous-growing hardy cultivar, which is very floriferous and bushy. It has wiry, arching growth with medium-sized mid-green foliage. The flowers are single, but can often contain extra petaloids, making them into a semi-double; they have a rich cerise tube and sepals and a dark purple corolla. The manner of growth allows training to almost any shape, but this plant excels when trained as a pyramid, looking like a Christmas tree with lots of sparkling decorations. It is

'Little Beauty'

an adaptable cultivar, also trainable as a pillar, espalier or standard. Hardy; Zones 6–7. Growth 65cm (26in). Bull, UK, 1901.

'Harlow Carr'

This floriferous cultivar is suitable for creating smaller-scale trained shapes. It has slightly lax upright and self-branching bushy growth with small dark green leaves against which the flowers make a good contrast. The flower is a medium-sized single with a pale pink tube, medium-length recurving pink sepals and a white corolla with red anthers. It will make a very pretty small to medium pyramid or pillar and is also worth trying as a small fan. Half-hardy; Zones 9–10. Johns, UK, 1991.

'Lillian Annetts'

This fuchsia quickly became very popular after its introduction because of its beautiful flowers and tremendous versatility. The flower is a small to medium double with a white tube striped green, white sepals and a lavender-blue corolla with patches of white and pink at the base of the petals. The upright lax growth is short-jointed and bushy, with small to medium mid-green foliage. This cultivar can be grown to most shapes, but it really excels

'Harlow Carr'

as a fan. It is very floriferous and continues to flower over a long period. Half-hardy; Zones 9–10. Clark, UK, 1993.

'Little Beauty'

This fuchsia is aptly named, with small to medium single flowers sparkling in its small, dark green foliage. The tube and sepals are pinkish-red and the corolla a lavender-blue. It has wiry and slightly brittle growth, and makes a good pyramid or pillar. Half-hardy; Zones 9–10. Raiser and date unknown.

'Lillian Annetts'

'Marin Glow'

An impressive fuchsia with medium-sized single flowers with a short white tube, white sepals with green tips and an imperial purple corolla fading to magenta. The flowers are striking and seem to glow, standing out from the medium-sized, mid-green serrated leaves. This cultivar is free-flowering, with upright and self-branching growth, and makes a very good pyramid or pillar, or a half or full standard. It is better to grow it in partial shade, as the sun will cause the corolla colour to fade. Half-hardy; Zones 9–10. Reedstrom, USA, 1954.

'Midwinter'

A smaller-growing cultivar which can be used for small pyramids, fans or standards and has small to medium single flowers with a white-veined pink tube and sepals and a white corolla inspiring its name. The growth is upright, slightly lax and self-branching, with dull dark green foliage. Half-hardy; Zones 9–10. Flemming, UK, 1990.

'Mrs Marshall'

This very old cultivar is still widely grown today. It has medium single flowers with a waxy cream-white tube and sepals and a rose-cerise corolla. The growth is vigorous and upright with medium-sized mid-green foliage. It makes a very nice pyramid-trained plant, but is also good as a standard. It was first introduced under the name 'Grand Duchess Marie'. Half-hardy; Zones 9–10. Jones, UK, probably introduced in 1862.

'Midwinter'

'President George Bartlett'

'President George Bartlett'

This cultivar, which is named in honour of a previous president of the British Fuchsia Society, has small to medium semi-double flowers with a burgundy-red tube and sepals and a dark aubergine corolla, fading with age. The growth is upright and vigorous, with a slightly lax habit, and the foliage is a glossy dark green. It is a very adaptable fuchsia: training to virtually any shape is possible, but it is particularly good as a fan, pyramid or standard. It can even be grown in baskets or hanging pots with care. Half-hardy; Zones 9–10. Bielby/Oxtoby, UK, 1997.

'Snowcap'

This fuchsia is so easy to grow that it should be in everyone's collection. It is highly recommended for beginners. The flowers are medium-sized and semi-double with a bright red tube and sepals and a white-veined red fluffy corolla. The growth is vigorous, upright and self-branching, with small to medium dark green foliage, and it is very floriferous. It can be trained into most upright forms – pillar, pyramid, conical or espalier – and is also very good as a standard or a permanent planting. Since it is not at all

'Snowcap'

lax, it does not work well as a fan or in a hanging basket. Hardy; Zones 7–8. Growth 61cm (24in). Henderson, UK, 1888.

'Suikerbossie' ('Sugarbush')

This cultivar has upright self-branching growth. Left to its own devices it will form a natural conical shape, so it is a good choice for training small pyramids, conicals and pillars. It is extremely floriferous, with small single flowers with a light green tube flushed pink, empire rose sepals with green tips and a lilac-violet corolla. The small dark olive-green leaves, which are lighter underneath, are sometimes hidden by the large number of flowers on the plant. Half-hardy; Zones 9–10. Brouwer, Netherlands, 1985.

'Waveney Gem'

This cultivar is strong-growing, self-branching and slightly lax with small mid-green leaves. It is very versatile and can be used in baskets, or trained as pyramids, conicals, pillars, fans and standards. The small to medium single flowers have a white tube and sepals and a mauve corolla. This useful fuchsia is well worth a place in any collection. Half-hardy; Zones 9–10. Burns, UK, 1985.

hanging baskets/pots

Fuchsias with lax, trailing or cascading forms of growth are excellent for use in hanging baskets and pots. Large double-flowered cultivars can be particularly spectacular.

'Ada Perry'

This is one of many wonderful large double-flowered trailing cultivars hybridized by Americans. Annabelle Stubbs is one of the greatest exponents of this art. This cultivar has a rather stiff habit, with large dark green leaves that are distinctively red-veined. The large double flowers have a scarlet tube and scarlet sepals with a darker shade underneath and a full corolla, which is blue-purple, streaked with rose. As well as being ideal for hanging baskets, it will make a splendid weeping half or full standard. This cultivar is rather tender and needs a heated greenhouse over the winter to keep it at its best. Tender; Zone 11. Stubbs, USA, 1983.

'Allure'

This Dutch introduction has large double flowers with a very long thin ivory-white tube, white sepals flushed pink, which are semi-recurving, and a full pink corolla. The foliage is mid-green and the growth is quite vigorous.

'Auntie Jinks'

'Caradella'

This cultivar does not enjoy full sun and fares better grown in semi-shade. Half-hardy; Zones 9–10. Moerman, Netherlands, 1991.

'Annabelle Stubbs'

This trailing fuchsia was named in honour of the famous hybridizer Annabelle Stubbs, so it certainly should be special. The flowers are a large full double with a light pink tube, reddish-pink sepals and a reddish-purple corolla. The foliage is large and mid-green. It makes an excellent hanging basket plant, where the large double flowers are an impressive sight. Half-hardy; Zones 9–10. Riley, USA, 1991.

'Auntie Jinks'

This trailing fuchsia is one that should be in everybody's collection because it is so adaptable and can be used in so many different places around the garden. The medium-sized single flowers have a pink-red tube with stripes, white sepals and a cerise-purple corolla with paler patches at the base of the petals. The colour of the corolla fades as the flower matures. It is extremely floriferous, with the pointed buds looking very attractive against the small mid-green foliage. Use it in hanging baskets, hanging pots or as a trailing edging plant in containers. It will also make a

good small weeping standard and can be used for other smaller trained shapes. Half-hardy; Zones 9–10. Wilson, UK, 1970.

'Caradella'

This cultivar has a striking flower that really catches the eye against the trailing mid- to dark green foliage. The medium single flowers have a pink tube and sepals and a violet-pink corolla. It is extremely free flowering. While it is well worth growing in all sorts of hanging containers, it really excels in hanging pots. Half-hardy; Zones 9–10. Delaney, UK, 1992.

'Cascade'

This cultivar is true to its name, with long cascading growths bearing many flowers at the ends. The flower is a medium single with a thin white tube flushed carmine, thin white sepals flushed carmine, which are held at the horizontal, and a deep carmine corolla. The foliage is medium to large, mid-green and serrated. It is a very good cultivar for mixed baskets and can also be grown on its own, although it tends not to flower much on the top of the basket. Half-hardy; Zones 9–10. Lagen, USA, 1937.

'Cascade'

'Cecile'

This is a very large double-flowering cultivar, which produces a lot of flowers for its flower size. The flowers have a pink tube, broad deep pink-red sepals and a lavender-blue corolla that is very full and frilled. The foliage is light mid-green, and the flowers and fat pointed buds stand out from this beautifully. This is a deservedly popular cultivar and well worth growing on its own or in a mixed basket. Half-hardy; Zones 9–10. Whitfield, USA, 1981.

'Dancing Flame'

This is a cultivar with rather unusual and distinctive flower colouring. The flowers are often smaller and semi-double at first, but after a short period of flowering they change to a medium-sized double. The tube is pale orange with darker stripes, the sepals are orange and darker underneath, and the corolla is orange-carmine, with the petal colour darker in the centre. It has stiff trailing growth with rather large mid- to dark green leaves, which set off the flower colour well. This fuchsia is ideal for use in mixed baskets. Half-hardy; Zones 9–10. Stubbs, USA, 1981.

'Emma Louise'

This relatively new cultivar makes a superb hanging pot, covering the growth with flower. The small to medium-sized double

'Falling Stars'

flowers have a pink tube and sepals and a powder blue and pale pink full corolla. The foliage is small and mid-green, and the growth is trailing and self-branching. It is also very good for mixed baskets and containers. Half-hardy; Zones 9–10. Horsham, UK, 1990.

'Falling Stars'

This cultivar has classically shaped flowers cascading off long arching, trailing growth with large mid-green leaves. The flowers are medium-sized, single with a pinkish-red tube, reddish-pink sepals and a turkey-red corolla.

'Frosted Flame'

It makes a superb half basket but also grows well in hanging baskets and pots. Pinch it well early on to make the best-shaped plant, as it is not naturally self-branching. It also makes a very good weeping half or full standard. Half-hardy; Zones 9–10. Reiter, USA, 1941.

'Frosted Flame'

This cultivar is a natural trailer, and will make a superb full or half basket. The flowers are medium in size and single with a white tube and sepals and a distinctive barrel-shaped flame-red corolla. The petals have a darker edge, and become lighter toward the base. The foliage is bright green and of a medium size and the growth is strong. Pinch it well early on to get the best shape. Half-hardy; Zones 9–10. Hanley, UK, 1975.

'Gerharda's Aubergine'

This trailing cultivar introduced from the Netherlands has small to medium single flowers. The flowers are a beautiful self-coloured aubergine, which is very dark when it first opens and fades to a more beetroot red as it matures. It is a vigorous cultivar with mid- to dark green leaves and will make an excellent basket or hanging pot. It is also ideal for mixing with white or light pink flowering cultivars. It is one of the best aubergine colours. Half-hardy; Zones 9–10. de Graaff, Netherlands, 1989.

'Emma Louise'

'Gloria Johnson'

This unusual trailing cultivar has very large flowers, 10cm (4in) long, which are extremely eye-catching. The single flowers have a long pink tube, long thin pale pink sepals held out below the horizontal and a bright rose corolla. The foliage is mid-green and the growth is strong with a vigorous trailing habit. This is one to try if you want to grow something that looks a bit out of the ordinary. Half-hardy; Zones 9–10. Bielby/Oxtoby, UK, 1994.

'Golden Anniversary'

Another superb cultivar from Annabelle Stubbs that is good for baskets, but may also be used in containers and as a weeping standard. The flowers are a medium to large full double with a greenish-white tube, broad white sepals and a dark violet corolla, which fades to a rich ruby colour. The foliage is medium to large, light golden-green in colour, and provides a beautiful foil to the flowers. This cultivar is deservedly very popular for its beauty. Half-hardy; Zones 9–10. Stubbs, USA, 1980.

'Golden Marinka'

This cultivar is a sport from the famous French cultivar 'Marinka', and it is probably one of the best trailing variegated foliage cultivars. The medium single flowers are similar to its parent, being a self-coloured red and contrasting well with the yellow, green and red foliage. The growth is not quite as vigorous as 'Marinka', but it is excellent for baskets or in mixed containers. The best foliage colours develop with a reasonable exposure to the sun. Half-hardy; Zones 9–10. Weber, USA, 1955.

'Greg Walker'

This Australian cultivar has a natural lax spreading habit and will make a beautiful hanging basket or large pot, but you can also grow it as a pot plant with the necessary support canes. The medium-sized double flowers have a white tube striped carmine-rose, white-carmine sepals and a very full violet corolla splashed red. The new foliage is a light green but matures to a mid-green later in the season. Half-hardy; Zones 9–10. Richardson, Australia, 1982.

'Harry Grey'

'Harry Grey'

This fuchsia should be in everybody's collection, and is very adaptable in use. The small double flowers have a rose pink-streaked tube, white sepals and a fluffy white corolla, but the colours will become pale pink in the sun. The foliage is small, dark green and very dense on the vigorous self-branching wiry growth. One of its advantages is that it stops like a single-flowered cultivar, often starting to flower eight to nine weeks after the final stop. It is suitable for all sorts of hanging containers. It will also make a good mini or quarter standard, or other smaller trained shapes. Half-hardy; Zones 9–10. Dunnett, UK, 1980.

'Haute Cuisine'

This wonderful Dutch cultivar is worth planting for its flowers and foliage, even though the growth is a bit untidy. The flowers are a medium to large double with a dark red tube and sepals and a wonderful dark aubergine corolla with red anthers and pistil. They make a terrific contrast with the medium to large pale to mid-green foliage. The best description of the growth is strong, spreading and lax. It is good for mixed baskets and containers and would make a nice weeping standard. Half-hardy; Zones 9–10. de Graaff, Netherlands, 1988.

'Gloria Johnson'

'Golden Marinka'

'Holly's Beauty'

This cultivar has large double flowers with a white tube, white sepals flushed pale rose and a pale lavender-lilac full corolla, an extremely pretty and unusual colour. The growth is trailing, with light to mid-green foliage, and it is very attractive grown in baskets or containers. The colour looks superb blended with other blues and whites in mixed baskets. The parentage is from a cross between 'Quasar' and 'Applause', and when first released it was subject to a trademark in California. Half-hardy; Zones 9–10. Garrett, USA, 1989.

'Irene Sinton'

This cultivar has large double flowers with a blush-pink tube and sepals and a pale lilac corolla splashed pink, with red veining on the petals. It has semi-lax growth with small to medium, mid-green leaves. It grows well in baskets and makes a very good hanging pot. Take very good care of it in the early stages and do not overwater, as it can be prone to botrytis. Half-hardy; Zones 9–10. Sinton, UK, release date unknown.

'Janice Ann'

This is a rather lax self-branching plant, which does well in hanging containers and makes a very nice hanging pot. The single flowers are small to medium with a turkey red tube and sepals and a violet-blue corolla, with bright pink anthers and pistil. They stand out well on the dark green foliage. The flowers often appear to sparkle, particularly if the container is in a shady position, catching the ambient light. It makes an excellent standard and is also good for growing in a trained shape, especially as a fan. Half-hardy; Zones 9–10. Holmes, UK, 1994.

'Kon Tiki'

This floriferous cultivar has rather wiry growth with small medium to dark green leaves and makes a nice hanging pot, but is also amenable to growing in baskets and containers. The medium double flowers have a white tube, white sepals flushed pink and a violet corolla with pink patches at the bottom of the petals. Not the easiest to find but well worth searching for. Half-hardy; Zones 9–10. Tiret, USA, 1965.

'La Campanella'

'La Campanella'

This free-flowering cultivar is very versatile, with wiry trailing self-branching growth with small mid-green leaves. It is best to pinch it well early on. It can be used for baskets, hanging pots and containers, but will also make an attractive small standard. The flowers are small to medium semi-double, with a white tube, white sepals flushed pink and an imperial purple corolla, which matures to magenta. It has been widely used for hybridization, especially in the Netherlands. Half-hardy; Zones 9–10. Blackwell, UK, 1968.

'Land van Beveren'

This vigorous sun-loving trailing cultivar does well in all sorts of hanging containers, and grows extremely well in a half basket. It is an easy cultivar for the beginner to grow. It is very floriferous and has medium single flowers with a long waxy white tube, waxy white sepals and a dark carmine corolla. The foliage is medium-sized and mid-green. It is vigorous enough to make a good half or full weeping standard. Half-hardy; Zones 9–10. Saintenoy, Netherlands, 1988.

'Irene Sinton'

'Marinka'

'Marinka'

This fuchsia, hybridized more than 100 years ago, is still a popular cultivar grown the world over. It doesn't have many faults, but the main one is the tendency for the leaves to mark and turn red with sudden changes in temperature, for instance when it is moved outside. The flowers are single, almost a self-red with a red tube, red sepals initially cupping the corolla and eventually held just below the horizontal, and a dull red corolla. The pretty flowers and buds look superb held in the mid-green foliage and the growth is naturally trailing, easily making an excellent hanging basket. This one is also worth growing as a half weeping standard. It was first thought to have originated in France in 1902, but now it seems it came from Germany some years earlier. Half-hardy; Zones 9–10. Stika, Germany, 1890.

'Mother's Day'

This Australian cultivar is a natural trailer with large, freely produced double flowers with a green tube striped white, white sepals with yellowish-green tips and a full corolla of frilled petals opening creamy white and maturing to white. The foliage is dark green on the upper surface and lighter green underneath. This makes an excellent basket plant and is a good choice if you want a very large white double to grow in mixed containers with darker cultivars. Half-hardy; Zone 10. Richardson, Australia, 1988.

'Multa'

This cultivar is a small-flowered single with a red tube, red sepals and a mauve-purple corolla. It is very easy to grow, and definitely a good one for a beginner to try, with lax growth and medium-sized mid- to dark green foliage. It is very free-flowering over a long period. As well as being an excellent half basket plant covered with flowers, it also makes a good standard with a lax habit, and can be used in mixed planting in any kind of container. Half-hardy; Zones 9–10. van Suchtelen, Netherlands, 1968.

'Novella'

This attractive cultivar has medium semi-double flowers with a long flesh-pink tube, long rosy-pink sepals and a salmon-orange corolla. The growth is rather lax with medium-sized, mid-green serrated foliage.

It grows very well in hanging baskets, hanging pots and containers, and will also make an attractive weeping standard. Half-hardy; Zone 10. Tiret, USA, 1967.

'Orange King'

This is one of a group of orange-flowered cultivars, and it makes an excellent basket fuchsia, with its trailing habit. It has medium to large double flowers with a white tube blushed pale pink, pale pink arching sepals and a very full corolla that opens orange, maturing to smoky salmon-pink with orange splashes. The foliage is serrated and mid-green, and the contrasting flower colour makes it quite striking. Half-hardy; Zones 9–10. Wright, UK, 1975.

'Panique'

This relatively new introduction is quite small-growing, but has a tremendous quantity of small single flowers. The tube is pink, the sepals are orchid-pink and the corolla is a deeper pink. The foliage is also small to medium in size and mid-green in colour. With its compact growth, this plant is excellent for a hanging basket or for use in mixed containers. Half-hardy; Zones 9–10. de Graaff, Netherlands, 2000.

'Panique'

'Pink Marshmallow'

This strong-growing trailing cultivar has very large double flowers with a long pale pink tube, broad pale pink reflexing sepals, and a full white corolla with loose pink-veined petals with some pink blushing depending on the amount of sun it receives. The foliage is a light green in colour and medium to large in size. This is a vigorous cultivar that will make a very impressive basket or can be used in mixed containers to add some stunning large flowers. In common with many white doubles, it is prone to botrytis, so take care with watering early in the season. Half-hardy; Zones 9–10. Stubbs, USA, 1977.

'Postiljon'

This vigorous self-branching and trailing cultivar is well worth growing, an easy cultivar for the beginner. It is early flowering and makes a good basket quickly. Its small single flowers have a short white tube flushed pink, and broad cream-white sepals flushed rose, held out over the rosy-purple corolla. The flowers contrast well with the small mid-green foliage as it hangs down from containers. It is also good for hanging pots, mixed containers and small weeping standards. Half-hardy; Zones 9–10. van der Post, Netherlands, 1975.

'Postiljon'

'Quasar'

'Princessita'

This older variety is still widely grown, for very good reasons. It has strong trailing growth with medium-sized mid- to dark green foliage and medium-sized single flowers with a white tube, long white narrow upturned sepals, flushed pink underneath, and a deep rose-pink corolla. It is very free-flowering and flowers over a long period. It makes excellent full or half baskets, as well as being a good filler for containers. Half-hardy; Zones 9–10. Niederholzer, USA, 1940.

'Quasar'

This is a large-growing spreading lax double, trailing owing to the size and weight of the flowers. The medium to large double flowers have a white tube, white sepals and a compact dauphin-violet corolla with white patches at the base of the petals. The foliage is light green and medium to large in size, and contrasts well with the unusual flower colours. This is a plant that is very good for growing in mixed containers. Half-hardy; Zones 9–10. Walker, USA, 1974.

'Red Spider'

'Red Shadows'

This is another lax cultivar from the American Waltz stable, with rather unusual flowers in a very nice colour combination. The large double flowers have a crimson tube and crimson sepals, which cup the dark burgundy-purple corolla, with crimson at the base of the petals. The flowers change colour as they mature, finally becoming a ruby-red. The foliage is mid-green with red veins. The growth is best classed as a lax bush, so it can be used in a hanging basket or as a pot plant with support. Half-hardy; Zones 9–10. Waltz, USA, 1962.

'Red Spider'

This superbly floriferous fuchsia is very vigorous, makes quite long stiff trailing growths with mid-green foliage, and is best pinched well early on. The medium single flowers have a long crimson tube, long crimson sepals and a rose corolla. It is an excellent cultivar, good for mixed baskets and containers. Half-hardy; Zones 9–10. Reiter, USA, 1946.

'Roesse Blacky'

'Roesse Blacky' ('Blacky')

This relatively new introduction from the Roesse stable, commonly marketed with the name 'Blacky', has a quite startling colour. The medium semi-double flowers have a red tube and sepals and a deep purple corolla that is almost black when it first opens. The foliage is small to medium in size and mid-green in colour, and the growth is lax and arching. It is very good for use in containers and baskets, particularly when the flowers are viewed from eye level. You could also try growing this fuchsia as a weeping standard, as its manner of growth is quite suitable for this shape. Half-hardy; Zones 9–10. Roes, Netherlands, 2002.

'Ronald L. Lockerbie'

When first introduced, this was promoted as the first yellow fuchsia; actually it is more of a creamy white. It had the honour of being named after Ronald Lockerbie, a prolific Australian hybridizer of fuchsias. The flower is a medium-sized double with a cream tube flushed carmine, white sepals and a cream to pale yellow corolla, fading to white. The foliage is medium-sized and light green, with quite long joints between the leaf nodes. This plant grows well in baskets and containers. Half-hardy; Zones 9–10. Richardson, Australia, 1986.

'Ruth King'

This is a stiff trailing cultivar with medium-sized mid-green foliage. The medium to large double flowers have a pink tube and sepals and a lilac and white compact corolla. This cultivar is very suitable for growing in the centre of mixed baskets and containers and well worth trying as a weeping standard. Half-hardy; Zones 9–10. Tiret, USA, 1967.

'Seventh Heaven'

This naturally trailing cultivar has medium to large double flowers, a white tube with green streaks, white sepals shading to pink, and a full orange-red corolla. It is an eye-catching and very floriferous fuchsia, with mid-green foliage and arching growth. It certainly makes a nice basket on its own, but is also excellent in mixed hanging containers. The flowers are at their best when viewed from eye level or slightly below, so this is another fuchsia that would be superb grown as a weeping standard. One that should be in everyone's collection. Half-hardy; Zones 9–10. Stubbs, USA, 1981.

'Seventh Heaven'

'Sophisticated Lady'

This cultivar is another American large white double-flowered and trailing cultivar very suitable for growing in baskets. The medium to large double flowers have a short pale pink tube, long and quite broad pale pink sepals, and a short, very full white corolla. The growth is naturally trailing, with small to medium-sized serrated foliage of mid-green with red veining. Half-hardy; Zones 9–10. Martin, USA, 1964.

'Southgate'

This cultivar grows in the manner of a lax bush with mid-green foliage, so it is ideal for baskets or as a pot plant with supports. The striking flowers are a medium-sized double with a pink tube, pink sepals which are paler above and darker underneath, and a powder-pink fluffy corolla with pink veining on the petals. Because of its slightly stiff manner of growth, it is amenable to other forms of training, such as a standard or even a fan. Half-hardy; Zones 9–10. Walker and Jones, USA, 1951.

'Southgate'

'Trudi Davro'

'Wave of Life'

'Susan Green'

This is a very pretty trailing cultivar with strong self-branching growth and medium-sized mid-green foliage. The flowers are single and of medium size with a pale pink tube, pale pink sepals with green tips and a coral-pink corolla. It can be grown as an excellent hanging pot or basket and is equally at home in a mixed hanging container. It will also make a superb weeping half standard. Half-hardy; Zones 9–10. Caunt, UK, 1981.

'Swingtime'

This cultivar is the classic basket fuchsia which everybody recognizes, and many gardeners have grown. The reason it is so well known is that it is one of the de facto standards against which other trailing cultivars are judged. The flowers are double and medium to large with a red tube, red sepals and a very full fluffy white corolla with red veining on the petals. The foliage is on the small side, mid- to dark green with red veining, and the growth is vigorous, wiry and trailing. It does very well in any type of basket or container, and can also be grown as an excellent weeping full or half standard. Half-hardy; Zones 9–10. Tiret, USA, 1950.

'Sylvia Barker'

This fuchsia has rather small flowers but they are numerous, with a long waxy white tube, waxy white sepals with green tips and a smoky-red corolla. The colours are quite distinctive and stand out well against the dark green leaves. It makes an arching, lax trailing plant that can be grown into an excellent half basket or hanging pot. This cultivar also grows very well in mixed containers and makes a superb weeping standard. Half-hardy; Zones 9–10. Barker, UK, 1973.

'Trudi Davro'

This is a relatively new trailing fuchsia, a good addition to the range of whites. The flowers are a medium double with a pale pink tube and sepals and a full white corolla, which stands out within the small to medium-sized bright green foliage. The pink becomes more intense grown in the sun. It makes a superb hanging pot, but is also well worth using in baskets or other hanging containers. Half-hardy; Zones 9–10. Raiser unknown, UK, introduction date unknown.

'Wave of Life'

This is an old cultivar, probably grown more for its foliage than its flowers. It has a small to medium single flower with a scarlet tube and sepals and a magenta-purple corolla. It bears splendid greenish-yellow and gold leaves, and the growth is lax but not especially vigorous. This fuchsia is probably best used in hanging pots or mixed containers for its leaf colour. Half-hardy; Zones 9–10. Henderson, UK, 1896.

'Wendy's Beauty'

This beautiful trailing cultivar has large double flowers, with a white tube and long white sepals flushed with rose, and an unusually coloured violet to pale purple full corolla. The flowers are produced very freely for such a large double and the lax growth has dark yellowish-green leaves, among which the flowers stand out well. Half-hardy; Zones 9–10. Garrett, USA, 1989.

'Wendy's Beauty'

triphylla fuchsias

Triphylla Group hybrids are quite tender subjects and have no frost hardiness. They mostly need a minimum temperature of 10°C (50°F) to grow on in green leaf through the winter and 5°C (41°F) to overwinter in a dormant state. Some may stand colder temperatures, but will take longer to start into growth again in the spring.

'Adinda'

This newer Triphylla cultivar is a slightly smaller variety with beautiful small single flowers growing in terminal clusters, the flowers being a salmon-pink self (the tube, sepals and corolla are all the same colour). The foliage is an attractive shade of sage green, with upright growth. It makes an excellent pot plant and a great summer bedder. Tender; Zone 11. Dijkstra, Netherlands, 1995.

'Adinda'

'Coralle'

'Billy Green'

'Andenken an Heinricht Henkel' ('Heinricht Henkel')

This cultivar, sometimes named simply 'Heinricht Henkel', is a beautiful lax Triphylla fuchsia with its medium rosy-crimson flowers growing in terminal clusters. The flowers make a beautiful contrast to the large dark foliage and it stands full sun quite happily. It can be used as a pot plant, but you can also try growing it in a basket, or as a lax standard. Tender; Zone 11. Berger, Germany, 1896.

'Billy Green'

This popular cultivar is a Triphylla type, rather than a true Triphylla. This means it has flowers growing from the leaf axils rather than in terminal racemes. The flower is very much a Triphylla shape, though a little fatter. The flower colour is a salmon-pink self and the growth is vigorous and upright with lovely olive-sage-green foliage. It will make an excellent specimen plant in a single season of growth. This is one for a patio as it happily stands full sun. Try using it as a summer bedder as well. Tender; Zones 10–11. Unknown, UK, 1962.

'Chantry Park'

This cultivar is rather unusual. It has short-jointed, bushy and slightly lax growth with medium mid- to olive-green foliage. It is still truly terminal flowering, with medium-sized flowers in terminal clusters. The flowers have a scarlet tube and sepals and a bright scarlet corolla, the sepals and corolla being a little larger in proportion to the tube than the standard types. It grows excellently in a hanging pot or basket. Tender; Zone 11. Stannard, UK, 1991.

'Coralle' ('Koralle')

This cultivar resulted from the work of the German hybridizer Carl Bonstedt, and is also known by the alternative German spelling 'Koralle'. It is a strong, upright grower with medium-sized flowers growing in terminal clusters. The flowers are orange-red self-coloured, with large, deep sage-green, velvety foliage. It tolerates the sun quite well but can wilt in very strong direct sun. It is not as frost shy as some of the other Triphyllas. Tender; Zone 11. Bonstedt, Germany, 1905.

'Firecracker'

This Triphylla is a truly variegated sport from 'Thalia', which is now widely grown. It flowers in terminal clusters, as does 'Thalia', and the medium flowers are orange-scarlet self-coloured, but it has beautiful leaves with a vivid olive-green and cream variegation with traces of red. Use it in pots or as a summer bedder, but be aware that it needs to be grown rather dry or you will lose it to botrytis. This cultivar is subject to breeder's rights protection. Tender; Zone 11. Fuchsiavale, UK, 1987.

'Insulinde'

This is a newer Triphylla hybrid with upright growth and lovely dark green shiny foliage. The medium-sized flowers are borne in terminal clusters with a tube of tomato-red, sepals tomato-red on the topside and vermilion-pink on the underside, and a tomato-red corolla. It makes a very nice pot plant and can also be grown as a summer bedder, tolerating full sun. Tender; Zone 11. de Graaff, Netherlands, 1991.

'Jackqueline'

This Triphylla cultivar has terminal clusters of medium flowers with a scarlet tube and sepals and an orange corolla. It has good upright growth with dark green velvety leaves, and is happy in full sun. Use it as a pot plant or a striking specimen plant. Tender; Zone 11. Oxtoby, UK, 1987.

'Mary'

This is another of Carl Bonstedt's raisings, and arguably one of the best Triphyllas in cultivation. It bears its medium-sized vivid crimson self-coloured flowers in terminal clusters. The tube is distinctly slimmer at the top and widens close to the flower. The growth is upright, self-branching and slightly lax, with large velvety leaves that are a beautiful shade of sage green. It is quite happy in full sun and makes an excellent specimen plant. It will also make a nice, slightly lax quarter or half standard, though great care is needed growing the stem. If it starts to flower while you are growing the stem, it will not grow any higher. Tender; Zone 11. Bonstedt, Germany, 1897.

'Insulinde'

'Our Ted'

This was the first white-flowered Triphylla cultivar, and it was named after Ted Stiff, a great fuchsia personality in the east of England. The growth is upright, with terminal clusters of medium white self-coloured flowers, though the corolla petals can have a touch of pink. The foliage is dark green and quite glossy. This is one for the experienced gardener, as it is not an easy cultivar to grow. Tender; Zone 11. Goulding, UK, 1987.

'Sparky'

'Sparky'

This new Triphylla cultivar is unusual in that the small flowers are thrown outward and upward in terminal clusters. The tube and sepals are dark blood-red, as is the corolla. It has upright growth and is short-jointed and very bushy, with small to medium (for a Triphylla) dark green leaves. It can be grown as a pot plant and would make a good quarter standard. It does very well when grown in a conservatory. Tender; Zone 11. Webb, UK, 1994.

'Thalia'

This is probably the best known of the Triphylla hybrids. It has strongly upright growth with medium-sized orange-scarlet self-coloured flowers borne in terminal clusters. The foliage is a dark olive-green, which shows the flowers off very well. This fuchsia is very often used in public park bedding schemes, as it makes a good show. It can form an excellent specimen plant and a good quarter or half standard. Once it starts flowering it doesn't stop until you have to cut it back in the autumn. It is a popular fuchsia, sold by most garden centres and nurseries. Tender; Zone 11. Bonstedt, Germany, 1905.

fuchsias in pots

Many fuchsia cultivars will make excellent plants for growing in pots, and these can be used for brightening up dark corners around the garden, for displays or for exhibition.

'Alaska'

This cultivar is a good upright grower with strong stems and striking large white double flowers with a white tube, white sepals tipped green, and a very full fluffy white corolla. The foliage is dark green, and when the plant is in full flower there is some arching of the stems caused by the weight of the flowers. This is one worth trying as a standard, and is ideal for placing in dull corners, where the white flowers will glow. It is worth considering for any collection. Half-hardy; Zones 9–10. Schnabel, USA, 1963.

'Albertina'

This is a strong-growing, self-branching plant, and will form a good bush or shrub with minimal shaping. The small to medium-sized single flowers have a white tube flushed rose, white reflexed sepals flushed rose and a flared lavender-rose corolla. The foliage is

'Albertina'

'Border Raider'

medium-sized, mid- to dark green. This fuchsia is very free flowering and makes a good pot or smaller standard. Try using it for summer bedding as well. Half-hardy; Zones 9–10. Netjes, Netherlands, 1988.

'Bealings'

This cultivar is an excellent choice for a medium-sized pot or as a small standard. The flower is a small to medium double with a white tube and sepals, and the corolla is very full, dark violet in colour, fading with age. The growth is upright, short-jointed and self-branching with small mid-green leaves and many flowers for a double cultivar. Half-hardy; Zones 9–10. Goulding, UK, 1983.

'Border Raider'

This fuchsia has made a big impression in the exhibition world since its introduction. The flower is a small to medium-sized semi-erect single with a deep rose tube and sepals and a white corolla with slightly

'Cambridge Louie'

scalloped edges to the petals. The growth is naturally shrub-like, with small to medium-sized light green leaves, and it is very floriferous. It will make a very nice quarter standard as well as being ideal for a pot plant. This cultivar does not overwinter well in a dormant state and is better kept in green leaf if possible. Half-hardy; Zones 9–10. Gordon, UK, 2001.

'Cambridge Louie'

This cultivar should be in everybody's collection as it is a vigorous grower and will easily form a large pot plant covered in flower. It seems to like direct sun as long as you keep the roots cool; in fact it actually grows better in the sun, forming harder wood that is not so likely to collapse under the weight of flowers. The medium single flowers have a pink-orange tube and sepals and a rosy-pink corolla, and they stand out well on the small, light green foliage. Half-hardy; Zones 9–10. Napthen, UK, 1977.

'Casper Hauser'

This cultivar is worth growing for the unusual flower colours. The growth is spreading, upright and self-branching, with light to mid-green foliage. It is a vigorous plant and grows quickly into an impressive shrub. The flower is a small to medium double with a cardinal red tube and sepals and a rather tight ruby-red corolla with lighter red patches at the base of the petals. Try using it in baskets as a centre plant, since it grows rather stiff and upright. Half-hardy; Zones 9–10. Springer, Netherlands, 1987.

'Cloverdale Pearl'

This fuchsia is very easy to grow as a pot plant, with its upright, self-branching growth and small mid- to dark green leaves. The flower is a medium-sized single with a white tube, pale pink sepals with green tips and a white corolla with red veining on the petals. This cultivar can also be grown as a summer bedder, and can be trained as a standard or other shapes. Half-hardy; Zones 9–10. Gadsby, UK, 1974.

'Cotton Candy'

This good strong upright-growing cultivar will make a nice shrub with medium-sized double flowers with a white tube, white sepals flushed pink and a fluffy pale pink corolla with cerise veins. The medium to large mid- to dark green leaves make a good foil for the flowers, which are freely produced for a double. It will make a large plant quite quickly, so it is also possible to grow it as a half standard. Half-hardy; Zones 9–10. Tiret, USA, 1994.

'Delta's K.O.'

This vigorous upright-growing cultivar will make a large bush or shrub quickly. The flowers are large and double with a cream tube, cream sepals flushed rosy-purple and much darker underneath, and a deep purple corolla. The foliage is medium-sized and mid- to dark green. The overall effect is very striking. Half-hardy; Zones 9–10. Vreeke-van't Westeinde, Netherlands, 1994.

'Doris Joan'

This cultivar is a strong-growing upright fuchsia with mid- to dark green, slightly glossy leaves, and rather unusual striking flowers. The flower is a small to medium-sized single with a cream and carmine tube, cream and carmine reflexed sepals with green tips and an unusual pale pink and lavender corolla with pronounced scalloped edges to the petals, giving the flower a distinctive shape. Half-hardy; Zones 9–10. Sheppard, UK, 1997.

'Doris Joan'

'Eden Lady'

This plant is a sister seedling to 'Border Queen' and has a similar habit of growth, namely upright, self-branching, bushy and short-jointed. It is easy to grow to a superb bush or shrub. The flowers are a medium-sized single with rose tube and sepals and a hyacinth-blue corolla, and they stand out beautifully among the mid-green leaves. Either 'Eden Lady' or 'Border Queen' should be in every beginner's collection. It is excellent either as a half or quarter standard, or in summer bedding. Half-hardy; Zones 9–10. Ryle, UK, 1975.

'Estelle Marie'

This cultivar is one of the upward-flowering types and therefore it is good for growing in pots, patio containers or as a summer bedder. The flower is a small single with a greenish-white tube, white sepals with green tips and a violet-blue corolla maturing to violet. It is extremely floriferous and has strong, stiff, short-jointed, upright growth with light to mid-green foliage. Use it as a single specimen plant or in mixed containers with other fuchsias or companion plants. This fuchsia's flowers look rather similar to little pansies, nodding in the breeze, making it a really good choice to use as a summer bedder, individually or in blocks. Half-hardy; Zones 9–10. Newton, UK, 1973.

'Cotton Candy'

'Heidi Ann'

'Frank Saunders'

This fuchsia has very pretty small single flowers with a white tube and sepals and a small lilac-pink corolla. The flowers are semi-erect, tending to stand out from the foliage. The growth habit is upright, bushy and self-branching with small dark green leaves. It forms a dense shrub very easily and is excellent as a pot plant, or try growing it as a beautiful miniature or quarter standard. Half-hardy; Zones 9–10. Dyos, UK, 1984.

'Gordon Thorley'

This is a strong, upright and self-branching cultivar with medium-sized single flowers with a pink tube, pink-rose sepals and a white-veined pink corolla. The plant is very floriferous, with mid- to dark green foliage. It makes an excellent pot plant, and is also very good for use in the border. Half-hardy; Zones 9–10. Roe, UK, 1987.

'Happy Wedding Day'

This Australian cultivar has large double flowers featuring a white tube, white sepals with rose-bengal colouring near the tube and on the sepal edges and a tight white corolla. The foliage is mid-green with serrated edges and the growth is upright, made lax by the number and weight of the flowers. It is advisable to add some canes as supports when growing in a pot, but it will make a spectacular plant. Half-hardy; Zones 9–10. Richardson, Australia, 1985.

'Heidi Ann'

This cultivar is a bushy upright-growing plant, which will make a very good specimen, pot plant or quarter standard for the patio or garden. It has medium double flowers with a carmine-red tube and sepals and a lilac-veined cerise corolla with a double skirt of petals and petaloids. The growth is self-branching and bushy, with small dark green leaves with a red central vein. Both of this plant's parents are hardy, and this cultivar inherits those characteristics, so it is worth trying it in the border. Hardy; Zone 7. Growth 40cm (16in). Smith, UK, 1969.

'Hidcote Beauty'

This cultivar, found by a British Fuchsia Society member growing at Hidcote Manor in Gloucestershire, has a medium single flower with a long waxy cream tube, waxy cream sepals tipped green and a pale salmon-orange corolla with pink shading. The foliage is medium to large light green, the growth is upright, slightly lax, and it is extremely floriferous. It makes an excellent specimen plant, a nice half standard and is well worth using as a summer bedder. It is also on the AFS list of gall mite-resistant plants. Half-hardy; Zones 9–10. Introducer Webb, UK, 1949.

'Hot Coals'

This fuchsia caused a stir when it was first introduced with its unusual flower colouring, aptly described by its name. The flowers are a medium-sized single with a dark red tube, dark scarlet-red semi-reflexed sepals and a dark aubergine corolla. The growth is upright, short-jointed and self-branching with mid- to dark green foliage. It will form a lovely pot plant with the minimum of effort. Half-hardy; Zones 9–10. Carless, UK, 1993.

'Igloo Maid'

This is an upright-growing cultivar with medium to large double flowers with a white tube, white sepals tipped green and a full white corolla with a hint of pink. The leaves are medium-sized and yellowish-green. It makes a very impressive pot plant, and is well worth growing. Half-hardy; Zones 9–10. Holmes, UK, 1972.

'Igloo Maid'

'Jomam'

'Katie Susan'

'Impudence'

This American cultivar is a naturally upright bush and makes a superb pot plant. The medium single flowers are unusual, with a light red tube, long light red sepals which are fully reflexed up around the tube and a white-veined rose corolla in which the four petals are almost flat when fully open. The mid-green leaves complement the flower shape and colour. This is a plant that is well worth trying, both as a pot plant and as an espalier or fan. Half-hardy; Zones 9–10. Schnabel, USA, 1957.

'Joan Goy'

This cultivar has erect flowers and will make a very fetching pot plant, but it needs hard pinching early on. The flowers are a medium-sized single with a white-pink tube and sepals and a lilac-pink flared corolla with pale patches at the petal base. The buds grow in clusters at the end of the stems and the flowers appear to be growing as they mature, but this effect is probably caused by the gradual flaring of the corolla. The foliage is small to medium in size and dark green in colour. It is a delightful cultivar, and well worth growing. Half-hardy; Zones 9–10. Webb, UK, 1989.

'Jomam'

This upright, short-jointed and bushy fuchsia makes a superb pot plant that can be really eye-catching. The flower is a medium single with a rose-pink tube, quite large rose-pink sepals, which tend to twist slightly, and a quarter-flared pale blue-violet corolla which matures to a light violet-pink. The vigorous growth is on strong stems with dark yellowish-green leaves, and it will grow to a large plant quite quickly. When growing it, take care to keep the roots cool, as it does not like being overheated. Half-hardy; Zones 9–10. Hall, UK, 1984.

'Katie Susan'

This quite new cultivar is a very vigorous grower. It is short-jointed, upright and bushy and will make an excellent pot plant quickly. The flowers are a medium-sized single with a rose tube and sepals and a flared cyclamen-purple corolla with lighter patches near the base of the petals. The foliage is medium-sized and an attractive light green colour. Its only real fault is that it tends to throw a single flower from each leaf axil, but it makes up for that with the number of branches and hence number of flowers. Half-hardy; Zones 9–10. Waving, UK, 2004.

'Kobold'

This fuchsia is a natural growing bush with small to medium semi-erect single flowers with a red tube and sepals and a bell-shaped violet-blue corolla. The growth is upright, bushy and short-jointed, with small to medium mid-green leaves. The plant will continue to flower over a long period. Half-hardy; Zones 9–10. Götz, Germany, 1990.

'Kobold'

'Lady Isobel Barnett'

This is one of the most floriferous cultivars, with as many as four flowers from each leaf node. The single flowers are small to medium in size with a rosy-red tube and sepals and a rose-purple corolla with darker edges on the petals. The growth is upright, self-branching and bushy with medium-sized mid-green foliage. It will make a good specimen pot plant or summer bedding plant. Half-hardy; Zones 9–10. Gadsby, UK, 1968.

'Lambada'

This is a compact, pretty cultivar, which is very useful for small pots. It has small single flowers with a pale pink tube and sepals and a mallow-purple flared corolla with white patches at the petal base. The growth is upright and compact with small mid-green foliage. It has a tremendous number of flowers, making it a great pot plant or small standard. It is also excellent for use in mixed plantings. Half-hardy; Zones 9–10. Götz, Germany, 1993.

'Lilac Lustre'

An attractive cultivar that has beautifully shaped flowers and fat round buds that hang in the bright mid-green foliage. The

'Lady Isobel Barnett'

medium-sized double flowers, which are freely produced, have a rose-red tube and sepals and a powder-blue corolla with ruffled petals. It makes an excellent pot plant, but prefers to be kept in a shady position. Half-hardy; Zones 9–10. Munkner, USA, 1961.

'Marcus Graham'

'Marcus Graham'

Another introduction from Annabelle Stubbs, this cultivar never fails to make an impact. The growth is upright, quite vigorous and self-branching and needs to be well hardened to support the large double flowers, which have a thin white to flesh-pink tube, long broad dusky pink sepals and a fully flared salmon-pink full corolla with orange streaks on the petals. The foliage is quite large and mid-green. This fuchsia will grow well as a specimen bush or standard as well as a pot plant. Half-hardy; Zones 9–10. Stubbs, USA, 1985.

'Maria Landy'

This cultivar has vigorous, upright and self-branching growth and makes an excellent compact specimen plant. It also grows well as a small standard, and can be used in mixed planting or for summer bedding. The flowers are semi-erect small singles with a pale pink tube and recurving sepals and a pale violet corolla, and they are prolific on the compact growth. The foliage is small and dark green, giving a perfect foil for the beautiful flowers to display themselves. It is well worth growing. Half-hardy; Zones 9–10. Wilkinson, UK, 1991.

'Lambada'

'Orange Flare'

This cultivar is perhaps one of the best orange-flowered fuchsias, apart from those in the Triphylla Group. It has an early flowering habit, and is a plant that will be quite happy in full sun, although the colours do benefit from slight shading. The flowers are medium-sized singles with a short thick orange-salmon tube, orange-salmon sepals and an orange corolla, lighter at the petal base and darker on the petal edges. The growth is upright and bushy with medium-sized mid-green foliage. It makes a good pot plant or standard. Half-hardy; Zones 9–10. Handley, UK, 1986.

'Patio Princess'

This is a vigorous and spreading self-branching bush, easy to grow, which as its name suggests will make an excellent specimen plant for the patio. It flowers early in the season with small to medium double flowers with a neyron-rose tube, neyron-rose sepals three-quarters recurving, and a flared white-veined red corolla. The foliage is small to medium, mid-green with a red vein in the leaf. It does tend to throw a number of semi-double flowers as well, but the sheer quantity of flowers produced will compensate for this. Half-hardy; Zones 9–10. Sinton, UK, 1988.

'Phenomenal'

This cultivar is a striking sight today, but it must have seemed really spectacular when it was first released in middle of the 19th century. It has large double flowers with a thin scarlet tube, broad scarlet sepals and a lovely indigo-blue corolla with cerise veining on the petals, which are paler at the base. The foliage is largish, serrated and mid-green in colour, and the flowers are freely produced for their size. It is still an interesting cultivar to grow as a pot plant, although the branches may need some staking to support the weight of the flowers. Half-hardy; Zones 9–10. Lemoine, France, 1869.

'Plumb Bob'

Use this vigorous upright cultivar as a specimen pot plant, a standard or in summer bedding. The flowers are large doubles with a pink tube flushed ivory, ivory sepals with a pink flush and a red corolla with mauve tones,

'President Leo Boullemier'

and they are quite numerous for their size. The foliage is mid-green and of medium size and the growth is sturdy and upright. Half-hardy; Zones 9–10. Goulding, UK, 1974.

'President Leo Boullemier'

This is a vigorous upright cultivar that will make a good specimen pot plant or a standard, and also grows well as a summer bedding plant. The flowers are medium-sized singles with a square white tube streaked magenta, white recurving sepals and a bell-shaped magenta corolla. The foliage is medium-sized and dark green in colour and inherits good features from its parents, 'Joy Patmore' and 'Cloverdale Pearl'. Half-hardy; Zones 9–10. Burns, UK, 1983.

'Rocket Fire'

This is a vigorous upright bush cultivar with unusual double flowers, which are medium in size with a magenta tube, dark rose sepals and a corolla with purple pleated outer petals and dark pink inner petals. The foliage is medium to large, mid-green, and provides a nice background foil to the flowers. It will make a good pot plant. Half-hardy; Zones 9–10. Garrett, USA, 1989.

'Roy Walker'

This cultivar is one of the better white doubles – the colours stay quite white even in the sun. The growth is upright and self-branching with medium-sized mid-green foliage; it needs to be grown hard (that is to say, outside as much as possible) to make the wood strong enough to support the flowers. The flower is a medium to large double with a white tube flushed pink, white-veined red sepals and a flared white corolla. This cultivar takes a long time from final pinching to flowering, typically 12 to 14 weeks. It will make a striking specimen plant or half standard. Half-hardy; Zones 9–10. Fuchsia-La, USA, 1975.

'Roy Walker'

'Sarah Eliza'

'Silver Dawn'

'Sarah Eliza'

There is some confusion over this cultivar. It is often listed as a trailing fuchsia, but it has growth which is more bush-like, and it is just the weight of the flowers that makes the branches hang downward. The flower is a medium to large double with a white tube, white sepals flushed pale pink and a full white corolla flushed pink. Like most whites the flower becomes pinker in the sun, especially the sepals. The growth is upright and spreading with light green leaves, and it is quite floriferous, making it ideal as a pot plant or in the centre of a mixed basket or container. A very nice double. Half-hardy; Zones 9–10. Clements, UK, 1992.

'Satellite'

This cultivar has rather an unusual flower, a medium to large double with a greenish-white tube, white sepals with green tips and a dark red corolla streaked with white. The growth is strongly upright and the flowers blend well with the medium-sized mid-green foliage, standing out in the sunshine. It will make a very striking pot plant for the terrace garden or patio. Half-hardy; Zones 9–10. Kennet, USA, 1965.

'Silver Dawn'

This is a strong, upright, bushy cultivar with medium-sized mid-green foliage that will make an excellent pot plant or a decorative half standard. It has medium-sized double flowers with a long white tube, broad white sepals tipped green and a beautiful aster-violet corolla. Half-hardy; Zones 9–10. Bellamy, UK, 1983.

'Snowfire'

This is another introduction from Annabelle Stubbs. It is a very striking fuchsia that will make an excellent pot plant, or can be grown in mixed containers. The flower is a large double with a pink tube, wide white sepals and a bright coral corolla with white patches, which are larger on the outer petals. The foliage is medium to large in size and dark green in colour. This fuchsia always attracts people's attention. Half-hardy; Zones 9–10. Stubbs, USA, 1978.

'Sunray'

This is one of the best of the variegated-leaf cultivars. It forms a slow-growing bush with the best leaf colours developed in the sun or bright conditions. Though it is grown more for its foliage than the flowers, they are not unattractive, being small to medium-sized single with a cerise tube, cerise sepals and a rosy-purple corolla. The foliage is medium-sized and has yellow, green and red colours in the leaf. This fuchsia will form an attractive smaller pot plant or blend well in a mixed container. An alternative plant to consider is 'Tom West', which is a little faster growing, but the leaf colours are not quite as good. Half-hardy; Zones 9–10. Rudd, UK, 1872.

'Thamar'

This eye-catching fuchsia cultivar is rather unusual, with upright growth and flowers held erect like little pansies. The flower is a small single with a white tube, white cupped sepals with a faint pink blush and a pale blue corolla with white patches at the base. The foliage is medium-sized and dark green. It is a very floriferous plant and the growth is upright, but not self-branching, so it benefits from early pinching. It stays in flower for a long time and makes a good specimen pot plant, container plant or summer bedder. Well worth growing. Half-hardy; Zones 9–10. Springer, Germany, 1986.

'Snowfire'

'Ting a Ling'

'Wilson's Sugar Pink'

'Ting a Ling'

This is an upright bushy cultivar, which is excellent grown as a shrub pot plant or as a quarter or half standard. It has a medium single flower with a white tube, white sepals three-quarters recurved and a white bell-shaped flared corolla. The foliage is medium-sized and mid-green and it grows well, although like many whites it can be prone to botrytis. Half-hardy; Zones 9–10. Schnabel-Paskesen, USA, 1959.

'Twinny'

This cultivar is quite a new introduction, but it is already very popular and makes an impressive pot plant or up to a half standard. The flower is a small to medium single with a red tube, pink-red sepals and white corolla with red veining. The growth is upright, self-branching, very bushy and floriferous with small mid- to dark green leaves. This cultivar does not do well in very hot conditions and prefers growing in a cooler climate. Try growing in clay pots. Half-hardy; Zones 9–10. Gordon, UK, 1999.

'Upward Look'

This upright vigorous bush cultivar has medium-sized erect single flowers with a carmine tube, carmine sepals with green tips and a pale purple corolla. This was the first notable cultivar with erect flowers released after 'Don Accord' in 1861. It has dull mid-green foliage and grows well in full sun, so it will make an excellent specimen pot plant, standard or summer bedder. Half-hardy; Zones 9–10. Gadsby, UK, 1968.

'Violet Basset-Burr'

This is a tremendously striking fuchsia with an aristocratic-sounding name and a fantastic flower. The flower is a large double with a greenish-white and pink tube, white sepals with green tips almost fully recurved and pink at the base, and a very full pale lilac corolla. The growth is upright and bushy, and the foliage is dark green. It will be at its best as a specimen pot plant or a full or half standard. This fuchsia is one that will turn heads and is well worth growing. Half-hardy; Zones 9–10. Holmes, UK, 1972.

'Voodoo'

This cultivar has spectacular large double flowers with a dark red tube, long dark red sepals and a very full dark purple-violet corolla with some red splashes at the base of the petals. The growth is vigorous, bushy and upright with medium to large mid-green foliage, but the plant needs to be grown quite hard, outside as much as possible, or staked to help support the very large flowers. It makes an excellent specimen plant in a container or large pot. Half-hardy; Zones 9–10. Tiret, USA, 1953.

'Wilson's Sugar Pink'

This vigorous cultivar is bush-like in habit, but can tend to become a little lax. If you grow it in full sun, this will help to keep it upright. The flower is a small single with a white tube shading to pink, pale pink sepals, and a mallow to pale pink corolla. The plant throws a tremendous number of flowers. The small to medium-sized leaves are an attractive light green. Half-hardy; Zones 9–10. Wilson, UK, 1979.

hardy fuchsias

When planted correctly outside, hardy fuchsias should survive winter temperatures down to -23°C (-10°F). The heights stated can be expected with temperatures down to -18 to -12°C (0 to 10°F).

'Alice Hoffman'

One of the smaller-growing hardy fuchsias, this cultivar has small semi-double flowers with tube and sepals both coloured rose, and a white, rose-veined corolla. The growth is wiry, spreading upright, and the foliage is small and bronze-green. A very nice compact growing bush, it does well at the front of the hardy border and is useful in the rockery. It will also make an effective small standard. This cultivar has an RHS Award of Garden Merit, awarded in 2002. Hardy; Zones 7–8. Growth 45cm (18in). Klese, Germany, 1911.

'Army Nurse'

A strong, upright bush with flared medium-sized semi-double flowers with a short red tube, red sepals and a mauve-blue corolla, the petals having a pink blush at the base. It is a vigorous grower with light to mid-green foliage, and will make a fair-sized plant with one season's growth. You can grow it as an impressive pot plant, or plant it out in the border as a summer bedder. This cultivar has

'Army Nurse'

'Baby Blue Eyes'

an RHS Award of Garden Merit, awarded in 1993. Hardy; Zone 7. Growth 105cm (41in). Hodges, USA, 1947.

'Baby Blue Eyes'

This cultivar has upright and strong bushy growth with small single flowers. The flowers have red sepals and tube and a dark lavender corolla, and the foliage is medium-sized and dark green in colour. It is very floriferous, and will grow well in the middle of a hardy bed. This cultivar has an RHS Award of Garden Merit, awarded in 2005. A very pretty cultivar. Hardy; Zones 6–7. Growth 90cm (36in). Plummer, UK, 1952.

'Beacon'

This is an old hardy cultivar with quite stiff upright growth and medium-sized single flowers with a deep pink tube and sepals, and a mauvish-pink flared corolla. The foliage is a darkish green with wavy serrated edges. Older specimens have very unusual bark on the wood. There is a sport from 'Beacon' called 'Beacon Rosa', where the flowers are the same shape but a self-pink. Hardy; Zone 7. Growth 60cm (24in). Bull, UK, 1871.

'Charming'

This cultivar is an easy hardy variety to grow, upright and vigorous with medium-sized single flowers with a carmine tube, well-reflexed reddish-cerise sepals and a rosy-purple corolla. The flower is the classic fuchsia shape and sits well against the medium yellowish-green foliage. This fuchsia will make a successful standard. It received an RHS Award of Merit in 1929. This cultivar is sometimes confused with 'Drame', but the flower of 'Charming' is longer and the growth is more upright. Hardy; Zones 6–7. Growth 70cm (27in). Lye, UK, 1895.

'Cliff's Hardy'

This upright and bushy cultivar has medium-sized single semi-erect flowers with a light crimson tube, light crimson-tipped green sepals and a campanula-violet corolla. The flowers are thrown up nicely against the small mid- to dark green leaves and it is a vigorous grower, ideal for a fuchsia hedge. Do not over-feed this one, as it will make growth at the expense of flowers. Parentage 'Athela' x 'Bon Accord'. Hardy; Zones 6–7. Growth 55cm (22in). Gadsby, UK, 1966.

'Display'

This excellent old exhibition-class cultivar is a strong upright and bushy grower with serrated mid- to dark green foliage. It has medium single flowers with a rose-pink tube and sepals, and a darker pink flared corolla. It is very easy to train and can be used for most forms of trained growth, including pyramids and standards. It is hardy in Germany and the Netherlands in Zone 6 and 7 regions. This is an ideal candidate for everybody's collection. Hardy; Zones 6–7. Growth 61cm (24in). Smith, UK, 1881.

'Dollarprinzessin' ('Dollar Princess'/'Princess Dollar')

Although still sold widely as 'Dollar Princess', research has shown the original name was 'Dollarprinzessin'. Attributed to Victor Lemoine, and introduced in 1912, a year after his death, it now seems it was first introduced in Germany by Kroger in 1910. It is a cultivar which, when grown in the border, will make a mound covered in flowers. It has medium-sized double flowers with a cerise tube and sepals and a full rich purple corolla, splashed red, with mid- to dark green foliage. It is one of the few double cultivars that, when planted as a

'Garden News'

hardy in cold areas, will still be in flower shortly after midsummer. It is at its best in the second or third year when grown as a pot plant, and it also makes a good standard. Hardy; Zones 6–7. Growth 40cm (16in). Kroger, Germany, 1910 (Lemoine, France, 1912).

'Empress of Prussia'

This old hardy cultivar was thought lost from cultivation, but a plant was discovered in an English garden in 1956, where it had been growing for more than 60 years. After propagation, Bernard Rawlings reintroduced it. It has medium to large single flowers with a scarlet tube and sepals and a corolla of reddish-magenta petals with a paler patch near the base. It is very floriferous, throwing up to four flowers from each leaf axil, with strong upright growth. Hardy; Zones 6–7. Growth 90cm (35in). Hoppe, UK, 1868.

'Garden News'

This is a good hardy double cultivar for the garden, with strong upright growth and mid green foliage. The double flowers are medium to large with a pink tube and sepals and a full magenta corolla with ruffled petals. It is reliable and quite free-flowering for a double. Hardy; Zones 6–7. Growth 61cm (24in). Handley, UK, 1978.

'Genii' ('Jeanne')

This is an excellent cultivar in all ways and should be in everybody's garden. It is one of the few hardies originating from the USA. It was originally named 'Jeanne', but is now much more widely known as 'Genii'. It has beautiful small pale green foliage, which becomes lighter in the sun. It has single small to medium flowers with a cerise tube and sepals and a violet corolla. Because of its leaf colour it seems to sparkle and stand out in the hardy border. You can also try it as a standard or a specimen plant in a large pot. Hardy; Zones 6–7. Growth 70cm (28in). Reiter, USA, 1951.

'Hawkshead'

This is a superb vigorous cultivar with small mid- to dark green foliage. It has small white self-coloured single flowers. It is that rare fuchsia, a white cultivar that stays white even in the full sun, with the flowers sparkling against the foliage. It is best placed at the back of the border because of its strong upright growth. In milder areas it will make a very large plant. Parentage was *F. magellanica* var. *molinae* crossed with 'Venus Victrix'. Hardy; Zones 6–7. Growth 120cm (48in). Travis, UK, 1973.

'Dollarprinzessin'

'Hawkshead'

'Howlett's Hardy'

This upright and quite vigorous cultivar has medium-sized single flowers with a red tube and sepals and a blue-violet corolla, with paler pink patches at the base. The foliage is medium to large in size, mid-green and serrated. The flowers are of a good size for a hardy and quite freely produced. It is a fuchsia to use in the centre of the hardy border, and will also make a nice pot plant. This cultivar has an RHS Award of Garden Merit, awarded in 2005. Hardy; Zone 7. Growth 55cm (22in). Howlett, UK, 1952.

'John E. Caunt'

A relatively new hardy introduced in 1994, this cultivar is a slightly spreading upright bush with bright mid-green foliage. The medium single flowers have a red tube and sepals and a flared magenta corolla. The flowers are held out well on the stem tips and it makes an attractive bush. This cultivar has an RHS Award of Garden Merit, awarded in 2005. Hardy; Zone 7. Growth 55cm (22in). Caunt, UK, 1994.

'John E. Caunt'

F. magellanica var. *gracilis*

'Madame Cornelissen'

This strong upright shrub has small semi-double flowers with a red tube and sepals and a milky white corolla with red veining on the petals. It is very free-flowering, with small dark green serrated foliage, which provides a nice contrast to the flowers. This cultivar is also suitable for small hedges. It has an RHS Award of Garden Merit, awarded in 1993. Hardy; Zone 7. Growth 60cm (24in). Cornelissen, Belgium, 1860.

F. magellanica var. *gracilis*

This is one of the natural species variants of *Fuchsia magellanica*, also known in the USA as 'Senora'. It has a vigorous, almost rampant, arching, slender growth with small, mid- to dark green leaves and single flowers that are slightly longer than those of *Fuchsia magellanica* itself. The flowers are small, with a red tube and sepals and a deep purple corolla. This plant makes a very attractive specimen hardy shrub because of its long, arching growth, and is also suitable for growing as a hedge. It has an RHS Award

of Garden Merit, awarded in 1993. Very hardy; Zone 6. Growth 90cm (35in). Lindley, South America, location unknown, 1824.

F. magellanica var. *molinae*

This is another of the natural species variants of *Fuchsia magellanica*, often sold as *F. magellanica alba*. In the USA it is known as 'Maiden's Blush'. This upright and vigorous shrub has small light to mid-green bright foliage, small flowers with a white tube and sepals and a pale lilac corolla (nearer white in the shade). Very hardy; Zone 6. Growth 120cm (48in). Espinosa, location unknown, 1929.

F. magellanica var. *pumila*

This natural variant of *Fuchsia magellanica* is the smallest of the group. It has very small flowers with a scarlet tube and sepals and a purple corolla, and it grows into a small mound with small dark leaves, covered with the tiny flowers. This fuchsia is best used at the front of the border or in a rockery. Very hardy; Zone 6. Growth 45cm (18in). Country of origin and date unknown.

F. magellanica var. *pumila*

F. magellanica var. *riccartonii* ('Riccartonii')

F. magellanica var. *riccartonii* ('Riccartonii')

There is some disagreement in the published literature about this fuchsia, and nurseries grow different fuchsias under this name. Often described as a *F. magellanica* variant, it was raised by James Young at the Riccarton estate in Scotland from a seed from 'Globosa' crossed with an unknown fuchsia, so more correctly it should be a cultivar. It is extremely hardy and vigorous, with small to medium single flowers with a red tube and narrow sepals held almost horizontally, and a dark purple corolla. This photograph is from the RHS garden at Wisley. Very hardy; Zone 6. Growth 120cm (48in). Young, UK, 1830.

'Monsieur Thiabaut'

This old French cultivar has medium-sized single flowers with a bulbous waxy red tube, broad waxy red sepals held horizontally and a mauve-purple corolla with paler patches at the base of the petals, which hardly fade in colour with age. The growth is strong, vigorous and upright, with dark green leaves, and it flowers early, profusely and fairly continuously. It will also make a nice standard, which will grow quickly to the desired height because of its strong and vigorous habit. Hardy; Zones 6–7. Growth 85cm (33in). Lemoine, France, 1898.

'Mr A. Huggett'

A compact bushy cultivar that is very floriferous. Its single flowers are small and stand out with a short red tube, horizontal red sepals and a mauve corolla with a pronounced purple edge and paler pink at the base of the petals. It is a good plant for the middle to front of the hardy border, with upright, bushy, self-branching growth and mid-green foliage. Hardy; Zone 7. Growth 68cm (27in). Huggett, UK, 1930.

'Mrs Popple'

This is an excellent old hardy fuchsia, often among the first to flower and the last to stop. It has vigorous upright growth with dark green serrated foliage and medium single flowers with a short thin scarlet tube, scarlet sepals and a violet-purple corolla with cerise veining. It is well worth growing in the hardy border, and is an exceptional cultivar for making a fuchsia hedge. This cultivar has an RHS Award of Garden Merit, awarded in 1993. Very hardy; Zone 6. Growth 120cm (48in). Elliot, UK, 1899.

'Nicola Jane'

This free-flowering bush cultivar has attractive medium-sized double flowers with a deep pink tube and sepals and a mauve-pink corolla, veined with cerise. The growth is upright and bushy, with mid-green foliage. It is a prettily coloured double-flowered cultivar that is very useful for growing toward the front of the hardy bed, and it also makes an excellent shape when grown as a shrub in a pot. It is a useful addition to the range of hardy doubles. Hardy; Zone 7. Growth 40cm (16in). Dawson, UK, 1959.

'Papoose'

This cultivar is one of the few hardies hybridized in the USA and has more of a spreading habit, growing twice as wide as it does high. It has small but profuse semi-double flowers, with a red tube and sepals and very dark purple corolla. The mid-green leaves are small and serrated. With its spreading growth habit, it will do well in a rockery. Hardy; Zone 7. Growth 40cm (16in). Reedstrom, USA, 1963.

'Monsieur Thiabaut'

'Mrs Popple'

'Prosperity'

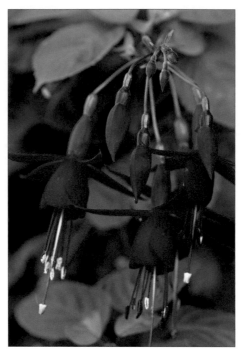

'Rufus'

'Prosperity'

This is a newer, vigorous, free-flowering hardy cultivar with medium-sized double flowers with a crimson tube and sepals and a neyron-rose corolla with red veining on the petals. It has strong upright growth with medium to large dark green leaves, and the flowers are a fair size for a hardy. This fuchsia is well worth growing in the hardy border if you want some double-flowered plants. This cultivar has a RHS Award of Garden Merit, awarded in 1993. Hardy; Zone 7. Growth 70cm (28in). Gadsby, UK, 1974.

'Reading Show'

This is another hardy cultivar with medium-sized double flowers with a red tube and sepals and a deep blue corolla, which is almost purple. It is an upright grower with mid- to dark green foliage and it is reasonably free flowering. Hardy; Zones 7–8. Growth 45cm (18in). Wilson, UK, 1967.

'Rose of Castile'

One of the oldest hardy cultivars still in cultivation, this fuchsia is still well worth growing. The flowers are a medium-sized single with a white tube with a green tinge, white sepals with green tips and a reddish-purple corolla with white patches at the base

of the petals. The growth is vigorous, upright and bushy, with mid-green foliage, and it is a very suitable plant for the middle of the hardy border. This cultivar is also worth trying as a quarter or half standard. Hardy; Zone 7. Growth 46cm (18in). Banks, UK, 1855.

'Rufus'

This is a strong-growing hardy cultivar, which develops naturally into an upright bush and is an early flowerer. The flower is a medium-sized single, almost a red self, with a red tube, turkey-red sepals and corolla. The foliage is mid-green with quite large leaves which are slightly serrated. It is suitable for the middle of the hardy border, or you could try it as a half standard. This cultivar is sometimes incorrectly named as 'Rufus the Red'. It is an easy one for the beginner to grow and highly recommended to try. Hardy; Zones 6–7. Growth 50cm (21in). Nelson, USA, 1952.

'Sealand Prince'

This hardy fuchsia is a strong grower, which naturally forms an upright bush. It has medium-sized single flowers with a pink tube, long pink sepals and a violet-blue corolla with paler patches at the base of the petals. The foliage is medium-sized and light green and contrasts nicely with the well-shaped flowers. This is a good plant for use between the middle and the back of the hardy border. Hardy; Zones 6–7. Growth 75cm (30in). Walker, UK, 1967.

'Rose of Castile'

'Tennessee Waltz'

'Sleepy'

This low-growing plant is one of the 'Seven Dwarfs' series raised by Tabraham in the Scilly Isles. It is listed as hardy, although there is a debate over just how hardy it is. The flower is a small single with a pale pink tube and sepals and a lavender-blue corolla, and it has small pale green leaves. The growth is compact and low, so it works best at the front of the hardy border, in the rockery or as an edging plant. Hardy; Zone 8. Growth 25cm (10in). Tabraham, UK, 1954.

'Son of Thumb'

This cultivar is another dwarf-growing compact plant, one of the sports of the cultivar 'Tom Thumb'. It is ideal for growing at the front of the hardy border or in the rockery. The flower is a small single with a cerise tube and sepals and a lilac corolla. The foliage is small and mid-green, and the growth is bushy, self-branching and compact. It makes a pretty miniature or quarter standard. This cultivar has an RHS Award of Garden Merit, awarded in 1993. Hardy; Zone 7. Growth 30cm (12in). Gubler, UK, 1978.

'Tausendschön'

This is a rather small, self-branching upright bush with small to medium well-shaped double flowers with a shiny red tube and sepals that almost look as if they have been lacquered, and a light rose corolla veined red. The growth is compact with small mid- to dark green foliage. It is an ideal fuchsia for growing toward the front of the hardy border and the rockery, or as a miniature or quarter standard. It will also make a very pretty double-flowered compact pot plant. Hardy; Zone 7. Growth 40cm (16in). Nagel, Germany, 1919.

'Tennessee Waltz'

This is a very nice hardy fuchsia. Although some references express doubts about its hardiness, testing in the Netherlands in an exposed Zone 7 site labelled it "Ned-H3 'goed winterhard' (truly winter-hardy)". Another factor, such as waterlogging, could have affected its hardiness in other trials. The flower is a medium to large semi-double, but often has enough petals to be a double, with a red tube, rose madder sepals and a lilac-lavender corolla splashed with rose. The growth is upright, self-branching and bushy, with medium-sized light to mid-green leaves. It is an easy one for beginners to grow and will make a nice bush or larger standard. Hardy; Zones 7–8. Growth 61cm (24in). Walker and Jones, USA, 1950.

'The Tarns'

This hardy cultivar has medium single flowers with a short pink tube, long pink sepals and a violet-blue corolla with paler rose patches at the base of the petals. The growth is upright and bushy with medium-sized dark green foliage. Hardy; Zones 7–8. Growth 55cm (22in). Travis, UK, 1962.

'Thornley's Hardy'

This fuchsia is, unusually for a hardy cultivar, a trailing plant. This makes it difficult to use in the hardy border, but it can be grown instead on the edge of walls or similar places where it can trail downward, and can also be used in baskets or hanging pots. The flower is a small single with a waxy white tube, waxy white sepals and a red corolla. The growth is lax, with small mid-green leaves. It is very floriferous and early flowering. Hardy; Zones 7–8. Growth 30cm (12in). Thornley, UK, 1970.

'Whiteknights Pearl'

One of this cultivar's parents is *F. magellanica* var. *molinae*, and the flowers are rather similar but somewhat larger, being a small to medium single with a white tube, pale pink sepals with green tips and a pink corolla. The growth is upright and bushy with small dark green leaves and light green stems. This fuchsia can also be used for training as pyramids and pillars. Hardy; Zones 7–8. Growth 100cm (39in). Wright, UK, 1980.

'Whiteknights Pearl'

summer bedding

Many cultivars can be used in the summer as temporary residents in the border and summer bedding plants. The following are among the best.

'Alison Patricia'

This cultivar is a vigorous, self-branching, upright fuchsia that is very floriferous and is excellent to grow as a summer bedder, pot plant or small standard. The flower is a small semi-erect semi-double with a red tube, pale rose-red sepals and a violet corolla. The foliage is medium-sized and mid- to dark green with compact growth. Half-hardy; Zones 9–10. Johns, UK, 1990.

'Anita'

This is a vigorous bush cultivar with small to medium single flowers with a clear white tube, clear white sepals and an orange-red corolla. The growth is upright and self-branching with medium-sized mid-green foliage, and it is very floriferous. It is an excellent plant for bedding use in the summer, being happy in full sun. There is another cultivar with the same name by Niederholzer, but this is a red and purple double. Half-hardy; Zones 9–10. Götz, Germany, 1989.

'Alison Patricia'

'Chang'

'Border Queen'

This is a striking fuchsia that should be included in any enthusiast's collection. With its good upright bushy and self-branching growth, with small to medium-sized mid-green leaves and red stems, it is excellent as a summer bedding plant, but will also make a lovely pot plant and is suitable for training into most shapes. The flower is a medium-sized single with a short, pale pink tube, narrow pale pink sepals tipped green and an amethyst-violet corolla with pink veins on the petals. Half-hardy; Zones 9–10. Ryle-Atkinson, UK, 1974.

'Chang'

This American cultivar, hybridized from *F. cordifolia*, has profuse small single flowers with an orange-red tube, orange sepals tipped green and a brilliant orange corolla. The growth is quite upright with small to medium-sized mid-green foliage. It thrives in the sun, and does well when planted out for the summer, with continuous production of the orange-red flowers. It is not easy to overwinter this cultivar, so it is worth taking autumn cuttings, which can be kept in growth over the winter in a greenhouse as a precaution against losing it during the winter dormancy. Half-hardy; Zones 9–10. Hazard and Hazard, USA, 1946.

'Cloth of Gold'

This old cultivar was a sport from 'Souvenir de Chaswick', and is grown more for its foliage than its flowers. It grows quite vigorously as an upright bush, and has beautiful golden-yellow foliage, which on ageing turns to bronze. The flowers are small singles with a red tube and sepals and a purple corolla, quite late to appear and rather insignificant. This fuchsia is ideal for creating a backdrop for other plants. Half-hardy; Zones 9–10. Stafford, UK, 1863.

'Dark Eyes'

This American cultivar grows as a slightly lax self-branching bush with small to medium dark green foliage and is excellent as a border plant in the summer. The flower is a medium-sized double with a short red tube, red upswept sepals and a tight violet-blue corolla with rolled petals. Try it combined with white-flowering fuchsias or bedding plants in the border for a bright contrast. This cultivar also works well as a weeping standard. Half-hardy; Zones 9–10. Erickson, USA, 1958.

'Dawn Fantasia'

This plant is one of a number of fuchsias originally derived from the cultivar 'Pink Fantasia', although it was in fact a sport from 'Rose Fantasia'. It is self-branching, bushy and upright in growth, and very free-flowering with small erect flowers. It makes an excellent fuchsia for summer bedding or a pot plant. The flower is a small single with a pale rose tube and sepals and a white corolla flushed pink. The foliage is a light to mid-green with a cream margin around the leaf. Half-hardy; Zones 9–10. Thornton, UK, 1999.

'Eternal Flame'

This American cultivar flowers profusely, normally well into the autumn, and with heat in a greenhouse or conservatory it will continue to bloom in the winter. The

'Dark Eyes'

attractive flower is a medium-sized semi-double with a salmon-pink tube, dark salmon-pink sepals tipped with green and a rose corolla streaked orange. The growth is strong, bushy and upright with medium-sized dark green leaves, which are a perfect foil to the flowers. It does extremely well as a summer bedder, but try it in containers or as a standard as well. Half-hardy; Zones 9–10. Paskeson, USA, 1941.

'First Kiss'

This Dutch cultivar has compact, upright and bushy growth, with rather square-shaped buds, and will make a nice pot plant or summer bedder. The flower is a medium to large semi-double with a cream tube, pale neyron-rose sepals tipped with green and a half-flared rose corolla with a very long pale yellow style. The foliage is rather small and dark green, giving a nice backdrop for the pale-coloured flowers. Half-hardy; Zones 9–10. de Graff, Netherlands, 1985.

'Golden Eden Lady'

This is a golden-leaf sport from the cultivar 'Eden Lady', sister seedling to 'Border Queen', with bright yellow leaves with green

patches, but retaining almost the same flower. The flower is a medium-sized single with a rose tube and sepals and a hyacinth-blue corolla. It makes a very good summer bedding plant, especially where a change in foliage colour helps the planting scheme. Half-hardy; Zones 9–10. Cater, UK, 1982.

'Hiawatha'

This Dutch cultivar is a compact-growing and upright bush that is very free-flowering. It makes an excellent small pot plant or summer bedder. The small single flowers have a short white tube flushed with rose, white sepals flushed rose and a dark red corolla. The foliage is small and mid-green in colour. This cultivar will take full sun quite happily and starts flowering very early in the season. Half-hardy; Zones 9–10. van Wijk, Netherlands, 1984.

'Ian Brazewell'

This is a very vigorous upright, bushy fuchsia that flowers very early and makes a good summer bedder, pot plant or standard. The flower is a medium-sized double with a claret-rose tube and sepals and a plum-purple corolla. The stamens hang down well below the corolla. The foliage is medium-sized and mid-green and is an excellent foil for the many double flowers. Half-hardy; Zones 9–10. Day, UK, 1988.

'Eternal Flame'

'Golden Eden Lady'

'Jack Siverns'

'Jack Siverns'

This is a superb cultivar from a hybridizer normally famed for his compact small-flowered introductions. It is a very strong upright grower, self-branching and extremely floriferous, and will make a very good specimen pot plant or standard, while also being ideal for bedding out in the summer. The medium-sized single flowers are of a classic shape and have a pink tube, pale pink upswept sepals flushed with aubergine and a beautiful tight bell-shaped aubergine corolla. The foliage is small to medium-sized and mid- to dark green. This cultivar is likely to be very popular as its fame spreads. Half-hardy; Zones 9–10. Reynolds, UK, 2001.

'John Bartlett'

This newish cultivar is very floriferous and frequently throws three flowers in succession from each leaf joint. The plant is also quite self-cleaning of seedpods. The flower is a medium-sized semi-erect single with a red tube and sepals and a white corolla with red veining on the petals. The foliage is medium-sized and dark green. It is worth growing this cultivar as a standard, or as a temporary summer resident in the border where it will flower all summer. Half-hardy; Zones 9–10. Humphries, UK, 2003.

'Ken Jennings'

This fuchsia is upright, bushy and strong, and will make a good pot plant or bedding plant for the border in the summer. It has a medium-sized single flower with a pink tube, rhodamine-pink sepals held horizontally and a deep purple corolla. The foliage is medium-sized and mid-green. Half-hardy; Zones 9–10. Roe, UK, 1982.

'Lydia Götz'

This German cultivar is popular as a summer bedder in many parts of Europe. It is an upright and bushy plant with medium-sized mid- to dark green foliage. The flowers are a medium-sized single with a red tube, red sepals held out horizontally and a very pretty lilac-blue corolla. Half-hardy; Zones 8–9. Götz, Germany, 1958.

'Minirose'

This plant is quite small and compact but also quite vigorous. It is early-flowering and continues to flower well over a long period. The flower is a small single, which is held outward and has a white tube blushed with rose, white sepals blushed with rose and a dark cyclamen-purple corolla. The foliage is small to medium in size and light to mid-green in colour. It will grow well in pots, will make effective smaller standards and also be quite happy in the border over the summer. Half-hardy; Zones 9–10. de Graaff, Netherlands, 1985.

'Minirose'

'Nice 'n' Easy'

This fuchsia is a good upright grower with self-branching, compact growth and is very floriferous and easy to grow, fitting its name perfectly. The flower is a medium-sized double with a carmine tube, carmine sepals held out horizontally and a white corolla veined carmine. The foliage is medium-sized, mid-green and quite narrow. It is excellent as a bedding plant in the summer, but will also make a good standard or pot plant. Half-hardy; Zones 9–10. Sinton, UK, 1988.

'John Bartlett'

'Other Fellow'

'Other Fellow'

This cultivar flowers extremely well and will make an excellent plant for the border over the summer, with its long continuous flowering period. The flower is a small single with a long waxy white tube, waxy white sepals tipped with green and a coral-pink corolla. The growth is upright and quite vigorous with medium-sized mid-green serrated leaves. It is also worth growing as a pot plant, a quarter or half standard or in mixed containers. Half-hardy; Zones 9–10. Hazard and Hazard, USA, 1946.

'Pink Fantasia'

Upon its first release, this cultivar made a tremendous impact, and it is now quite widely grown both as an exhibition plant and for garden displays. The medium-sized erect single flowers have a pinkish-red tube and sepals and a violet to mauve corolla. The growth is upright and bushy with medium-sized mid- to dark green foliage, and it has many flowers over a long period. Because of its erect flowering habit it makes an excellent plant for the summer border, but it will also make a striking standard or pot plant, which at its peak of flowering almost makes the leaves invisible. Half-hardy; Zones 9–10. Webb, UK, 1989.

'Rose Fantasia'

This cultivar is a sport of 'Pink Fantasia', and perhaps this one is actually more suited to its parent's name. It has almost the same growth habit as its parent, but the flower is a much softer colour. It has a medium erect single flower with a deep pink tube and sepals and a pale pink corolla with a hint of mauve. The foliage is still a mid-green, a shade or two lighter than 'Pink Fantasia', and it still has a very strong flowering habit. Again, it is excellent for use in the border, as a pot plant or standard. Half-hardy; Zones 9–10. Wilkinson, UK, 1991.

'Ted Sweetman'

This cultivar from New Zealand, named after a well-known fuchsia personality there, will make a very nice pot plant or a bedding plant for the border in the summer. The flower is a medium-sized double with a cream tube, cream sepals flushed green and pink and a violet corolla flushed pink. The growth is upright and bushy and the foliage is medium to large and a shade of greyish-green. Half-hardy; Zones 9–10. Sharpe and Proffitt, New Zealand, 1988.

'Walz Jubelteen'

This is another of the erect-flowering fuchsias, a strong upright bushy grower that is quite happy in full sun and is extremely floriferous. The flower is a small erect single with a pale pink tube, pale pink sepals with green tips and a pinkish-orange corolla which is flared almost flat when fully open. The foliage is a medium-sized light to mid-green. It is excellent as a specimen pot plant or for use as a bedding plant in the summer. Half-hardy; Zones 9–10. Waldenmaier, Netherlands, 1990.

'White Ann'

This cultivar is a sport from 'Heidi Ann' – it shows the same growth characteristics, with different flower colours. Note that an almost identical sport named 'Heidi Weiss' is separately registered. The growth is upright and bushy, with mid- to dark green foliage, and the flower is a medium-sized double with a crimson tube and sepals, and a white, crimson-veined corolla. It is well worth growing in the border or in pots. Half-hardy; Zones 8–9. Wills-Atkinson, UK, 1972.

'Pink Fantasia'

encliandras and unusual cultivars

The following are some interesting Encliandra hybrids and other unusual fuchsia plants with different flowers.

'Cinnabarina'

This Encliandra hybrid is an old cultivated form of *F. bacillaris* and is quite a vigorous grower, becoming untidy when grown in a greenhouse, but forming a compact bush in the hardy border. The flower is a tiny single with an orange tube, orange-red sepals and an orange corolla. The foliage is small and mid-green in colour. This is a good small hardy plant for use in a rockery. Hardy; Zones 7–8. Growth 45cm (18in). Raiser unknown, introduced c.1829.

'Delta's Drop'

This Dutch cultivar is an upright and bushy grower with mid- to dark green foliage that will benefit from early pinching. The unusual, eye-catching flower is a small to medium single with a red tube and sepals and a purple corolla with a red base to the petals, which become petaloids growing as part of the outer anthers as the flower matures. This fuchsia should be grown in the shade to get the best colours, as it can be bleached by too much sun. Half-hardy; Zones 9–10. Vreeke/van Westeinde, Netherlands, 1994.

'Marlies de Keijzer'

This fuchsia is an Encliandra hybrid, specifically a cross between *F. encliandra* and *F. thymifolia* subsp. *thymifolia*. It has tiny single flowers with a red tube, sepals and corolla, which sit among the rather attractive tiny grey-green shiny foliage. The growth is slightly more compact than that of Encliandra hybrids in general, probably due to the *F. thymifolia* parentage. Half-hardy; Zones 9–10. de Keijzer, Netherlands, 1999.

'Martin's Yellow Surprise'

This unusual tender cultivar is an interspecies cross of *F. piloensis* x *F. fulgens* and forms a large-growing bush. The flowers are a good-sized Triphylla type — while not growing as true terminal clusters, they are concentrated at the ends of the branches. The tube and sepals are green-yellow, though they can take on a pink blush in full sun, and the corolla is green-yellow, though always partially hidden by the sepals. Its growth is upright and quite vigorous with large felt-like mid-green leaves. As the plant is quite tender, it needs a well-heated greenhouse over the winter. It is an unusual plant which can be grown as a specimen on the patio in the summer. Tender; Zone 11. Beije, Netherlands, 1995.

'Martin's Yellow Surprise'

'Miniature Jewels'

This Encliandra hybrid has a natural trailing, self-branching manner of growth with tiny serrated green leaves and can be trained in a number of ways. The flowers are tiny singles with a rose tube, rose-white sepals and a whitish-pink corolla. As the flower matures, the sepals and the corolla darken to a dark pink to red, giving the visual impression of alternating flower colours. Half-hardy; Zones 9–10. Francesca, USA, 1976.

'Marlies de Keijzer'

'Miniature Jewels'

'Rose Quartet'

'Neopolitan'

This Encliandra hybrid is a bit unusual since it has flowers that can be red, pink or white, all growing at the same time, which creates a striking effect. The typical flower is a tiny single, but slightly larger than other Encliandra cultivars, with a red tube and sepals and a pinkish-white corolla. The growth is very thin and wiry, with tiny mid- to dark green fern-like foliage, and it is an excellent cultivar to use as a topiary subject. Half-hardy; Zones 9–10. Clark, UK, 1984.

'Nettela'

This fuchsia was a sport from the cultivar 'Chang' and shares similar growth characteristics, being upright and strong-growing with mid-green foliage. It is distinguished by the flower, which is a small to medium single with a short dark red tube, dark red sepals and a violet-red corolla where the petals are petaloids growing as part of the outer anthers. Half-hardy; Zones 9–10. Francesca, USA, 1973.

'Rose Quartet'

This new cultivar with its very unusual flower created a stir when it was first released in the USA, and is now available in other countries. The breeder assigned the rights to Planthaven Inc. in the USA, where it is subject to a US plant patent. The flower is a small to medium erect single with a pink tube and sepals and a rose corolla; the petals are petaloids growing as part of the outer anthers, which rapidly extend when the bud opens. The growth is upright, self-branching and bushy and it will grow to about 61cm (2ft) in a year from a small plant. In the patent, it is claimed to be hardy down to Zone 9, but treat it as half-hardy until more details are known. Half-hardy; Zones 9–10. Spanton, UK, 2006.

'Tarra Valley'

This unusual cultivar is another inter-species cross between *F.* x *colensoi* and *F. splendens* and is one for the collector. The buds are yellow-green and the flowers are small single with a long light greenish-yellow tube, short greenish-white sepals and an unusual dark red-purple corolla. The growth is upright and bushy with light green foliage, but it is quite slow-growing. It is reputed to flower quite well in the winter. Half-hardy; Zones 9–10. Felix, Netherlands, 1987.

'Variegated Lottie Hobbie'

This Encliandra hybrid was a sport from 'Lottie Hobbie', and is reasonably vigorous and self-branching, with attractive tiny silvery-cream and green foliage. The profuse flowers are tiny singles with a crimson tube, crimson sepals tipped pink and a crimson corolla. It is very eye-catching and hardy in more sheltered areas. Borderline hardy; Zones 8–9. Growth 61cm (2ft). Raiser and introduction date unknown.

'Waldfee'

This Encliandra hybrid is a strong grower with rather matt mid-green foliage, large for an Encliandra, which will form a lax upright bush or can be persuaded to trail effectively in a basket. The flowers are tiny singles with a lilac-pink tube, lilac-pink sepals and a pale lilac-pink corolla. This is an ideal plant for fuchsia topiary, and is hardy in more sheltered areas. Borderline hardy; Zones 8–9. Travis, UK, 1973.

'Walz Tuba'

This is an unusual Dutch cultivar that grows very strongly upright, and becomes quite tall. It would be ideal grown as a standard. It has medium to large dark green foliage and is noted for its beautiful long flowers. The flower is a single with a long thin red tube 6cm (2⅜in) long, small red sepals tipped with green and a small tyrian purple corolla. Half-hardy; Zones 9–10. Waldenmaier, Netherlands, 1987.

'Variegated Lottie Hobbie'

CALENDAR
of care

Fuchsias are easy to grow and will flourish with the right attention during the different seasons of the year. The calendar of care gives a seasonal guide of what needs doing and when for the best results, ensuring that you will get a wonderful display of colour in the summer.

The calendar describes the best time to carry out important tasks, such as encouraging dormant plants back into life, re-potting shooting plants, taking cuttings and planting up hanging baskets and containers, all shown in a seasonal format. It has tips for maintaining a hardy fuchsia bed and ways to keep fuchsias at their best through the summer, and gives details of how to prepare fuchsias for the winter storage period.

Left In midsummer, the stunning large double flowers of the fuchsia 'Marcus Graham' look fantastic. They have a waxy white tube, broad white sepals with a pink flush, and a full salmon-pink corolla with lighter splashes.

Above The versatile fuchsia 'Lillian Annetts' can be brought into flower in the late spring by using a heated greenhouse. The small to medium double flowers are white and lavender-blue, with patches of white and pink.

spring care

Spring is often the most exciting time for the fuchsia grower, with many things to do and the fuchsias developing rapidly. You may be taking cuttings, re-potting plants, visiting nurseries to buy new and replacement plants, shaping and growing on fuchsias and planting up baskets and containers.

Above The fuchsia 'Irene Sinton' needs removal of yellowing leaves and careful watering in the spring to avoid botrytis. This trailing cultivar has large double flowers with pink sepals and a pale lilac corolla splashed with pink, with red veining on the petals.

During this season, fuchsias will be growing very quickly. If you are not careful, you can end up rushing from one project to the other, having to look after far more cultivars than you ever intended to grow. Once you are successful at taking cuttings, you may have too many healthy new plants, and it is very difficult to throw any of them away. Take heed of the advice of an experienced fuchsia grower, and stick to the plan you made in the winter.

IN THE GREENHOUSE

In the early spring, temperatures in the greenhouse can vary widely. On sunny days, the greenhouse reaches internal temperatures of more than 25°C (77°F), while at night temperatures can still drop below freezing. Some shading will be required on the inclined glass that faces the sun to prevent scorching of young plants. Fuchsias will be growing very strongly and need pinching, potting on and turning, but don't forget that any plants needed for early flowers in the garden will take 10–12 weeks from the last pinch to begin flowering. If there are any overwintered plants that were not re-potted in the late winter, these should be done in early spring, potting down if necessary.

Continue to take cuttings of plants you want to propagate, especially those that you bought recently. Move plants outside on suitable days to start the hardening-up process. Start to plant up containers ready for putting out permanently when all danger of frost has passed. Grow on any plants that you are training as standards or other shapes, remembering to re-pot them, loosen their ties and remove the side shoots or pinch them out when required to maintain the shape.

Watch the plants closely for signs of pests and diseases, since at this time of year infestations can start. Aphids, in particular, can very rapidly infest plants and it is better to catch them early. Toward the end of the spring, as the day length gets close to the maximum, apply additional shading to reduce the temperatures in the greenhouse.

potting on

1 Use a smaller pot inside the next-sized pot as a mould and fill the gap with potting compost (soil mix). Gently lift out the inner pot.

2 Knock the plant out of its pot and drop it into the prepared mould. Tap on the ground to settle the contents and gently water in.

THE HARDY BORDER

If you have plants in the hardy border that you have not cut back in late winter, prune them in the early spring when conditions are good and green shoots are appearing from the base of the plant. Clean out any germinating weeds from the border, give it a dressing of a general fertilizer, and hoe a mulch of compost into the soil surface. If there are any inter-planted bulbs, delay the hoeing until you are sure where they are to avoid damaging the shoots. If you have any spring-flowering shrubs among the fuchsias, wait until they have finished flowering, then prune them back to the desired shape and size, remembering how much growth they will make in the summer. Watering is not normally necessary except in exceptionally dry periods. Toward the end of the spring, when all danger of frosts has passed, plant new hardy fuchsias to fill any gaps, or replace those that have not survived the winter, remembering the design.

THE GARDEN

Plant out greenhouse fuchsias that have been properly hardened off in their required positions at the end of the spring when the danger of frost has passed. Be ready to protect them with fleece if there is an unseasonable cold snap.

WARMER CLIMATES

By this time in the season, the plants are growing very strongly, and may already be in flower. Staking and tying, watering, feeding and mulching permanently planted specimens are the main tasks. The other major task is to provide extra shading in the greenhouse by the use of shade netting or similar protection against the heat of the sun.

THE SHADEHOUSE

This resource, which is essential in warmer climates, comes into its own at the end of the spring and allows pot plants to be grown when the temperatures regularly climb into the mid-30s Celsius (mid-90s Fahrenheit). It provides some shade from the sun, and a more humid atmosphere. Care will be needed in watering, feeding and turning the pot plants, watering the gravel base to increase humidity and cleaning up any dropped leaves to avoid disease.

Above The small red-and-purple-flowered hardy cultivar 'David' is easy to bring into flower in the spring using a greenhouse. Many other hardy single-flowered cultivars treated in this way can be encouraged to flower early in the year.

Left Standing plants outside on mild spring days is important to harden up the growth. This miniature standard of the hardy cultivar 'Tom Thumb' has been put out in the open air on a bright day to kick-start this process.

autumn care

The autumn season is a busy one. This is the time to preserve your fuchsia collection by preparing your cultivars for the rigours of winter. There are different methods and techniques that can be used depending on the facilities you have at your disposal and the local winter climate in your area.

Above With proper care, hardy cultivars such as 'Richard John Carrington' will continue flowering well into autumn. This cultivar has single flowers of bright cerise and blue-violet.

These guidelines are written for those readers who live in areas of the world that have frost in the winter, but for those who live in frost-free areas, the autumn season means simply pruning your plants to induce a dormant period and ensure that you have a bushy plant with fresh growth for the next year.

GENERAL AUTUMN TASKS

The first recommendation is to treat all the pot plants you plan to overwinter in their current pots with a proprietary treatment for vine weevil. This will destroy any vine weevil eggs and larvae that might eat the root structure over the winter. An alternative is to pot back plants before putting away for the winter, removing any vine weevil. Potting back gives the plants fresh compost and encourages new, healthy root systems. You can also do this in the winter or early spring when conditions are suitable.

Take cuttings from any plants cut back at the end of the summer when they have made new shoots, and from any other cultivars you want to keep if you can find suitable non-flowering shoots.

Clean the greenhouse and staging, then sterilize it, clean the glass and remove the shading. Put back the insulation, if necessary, and check that the heating system is in good working order.

PREPARING PLANTS FOR DORMANCY

In mid-autumn, dry out any fuchsias you wish to store in a dormant state over the winter. When they are quite dry, cut them back by about two-thirds, and remove any remaining leaves. Leave the cut stems to heal over for a few days before watering again. If any stems continue to bleed sap, lay the pots on their sides until the bleeding has stopped so that the sap does not run back down the stems,

potting back

1 Stop watering the selected plant until it has become quite dry. Knock it out of the 15cm (6in) pot, then remove as much of the old potting compost (soil mix) as possible.

2 The plant now has only a small amount of soil and the main roots left on it.

3 Put the plant into the smallest pot it will fit into, in this case an 11cm (4¼in) pot.

4 Fill the new pot with fresh potting compost. Push it down well, ensuring that you fill all the gaps, then water in sparingly.

cutting back a hanging pot

1 Leave the hanging pot outside, allowing exposure to a few light frosts. Bring the pot into the greenhouse to dry out for a few days before pruning.

2 Using a sharp pair of secateurs, cut off all the long growths, plus any that are crossing each other or are weak or damaged.

3 When the pruning is completed, the plants have been cut back to the edge of the pot and form a dome shape over the top of the pot.

causing rot. Spray the remaining wood and soil surface with a combined insecticide and fungicide to kill any overwintering pests or spores.

Store the plants for the winter in the greenhouse, either on the benches if the area is kept frost free, or on the floor under the staging if it is heated to a minimum of 5°C (41°F). If you do not have a greenhouse, store them in a frost-free shed, cellar or garage, wrapping them in paper if necessary to keep the frost away.

Trained shapes that are to be stored in a dormant state in the greenhouse can be treated in a similar way, though the pruning needs to be appropriate to the shape. Clean off all the leaves and spray the wood with a suitable treatment against red spider mite, which tends to overwinter in the bark of old specimens. Trained shapes that are to be kept in green leaf should be sprayed to kill any insects, moved into the heated greenhouse in good time before the frosts and kept ticking over. These shapes are best stored standing upright.

LATE AUTUMN TASKS

When the first frosts are threatening, break up the hanging baskets, checking for any signs of vine weevil, and cut back and pot up any cultivars you want to keep for the next year. These plants are also very good for encouraging into growth for early cuttings in a heated greenhouse. Treat any plantings in mixed pots, troughs and containers in the same way, while specimen plants can be simply cut back and overwintered in the same pot.

When the first frosts have blackened the leaves of any non-hardy cultivars growing in the borders that you want to keep for the following year, lift the plants, cut back the stems by one-half to two-thirds, remove the dead leaves, then pot them up and store them with good ventilation for a few days, and finally place them in storage. Lastly, clear away the dead leaves and compost them unless the plants have suffered from significant fuchsia rust during the season, in which case the leaves should be burned or disposed of.

Above Triphylla fuchsias will flower right through the autumn until the first frosts. Continue feeding the plants to maintain vigorous flowering.

Below This weathered terracotta (clay) pot planted with a hardy fuchsia will continue to flower well into the autumn. Keep removing seedpods to help it maintain this.

treating against vine weevil

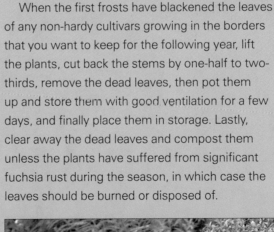

1 Pour the diluted emulsion of the proprietary treatment into a clean small watering can. Carefully read the instructions before use.

2 Apply the treatment as a soil drench to the pots. Stand the pot in a plant saucer to catch any drainage and allow it to re-absorb.

winter care

At this time of year, most fuchsias are stored away in their dormant state, or settled in the greenhouse, just ticking over in green leaf. It is a good time to sit back and browse through the catalogues and nursery websites. You may also want to tackle the more energetic task of preparing the ground for new hardy fuchsia beds.

During the previous season, you will probably have seen and made note of fuchsia cultivars you would like to try. Obtain catalogues from your favourite nurseries and read through the descriptions of the plants. Many nurseries now have their catalogues available on the internet, and are happy to take orders this way, or by letter or email. If you want to experiment with any of the new cultivars, make sure you order early, as there is often a limited supply.

THE HARDY BED

When frost has killed and removed the leaves from the stems in the hardy fuchsia beds, cut back any of the growth that is not woody. This is usually about the last third of the last season's growth. In very cold areas or for fuchsias you planted in the previous season, draw some soil up over the stems and add some extra winter protection in the form of dry leaves, straw or similar materials.

In milder areas, the end of the winter is the time to prune fuchsias back hard as they start to make growth, before the stems are growing so strongly that they will bleed when pruned. In colder areas, this is a job for the early spring.

IN THE GREENHOUSE

For a frost-free greenhouse, maintain a minimum temperature of 1°C (34°F). For a heated greenhouse, which will keep most fuchsias ticking over in green leaf and protect more tender cultivars like Triphyllas in their dormant states, keep a minimum of 5°C (41°F). It is possible to use higher temperatures,

Left Placing plants under the staging in a heated greenhouse in winter will keep them in green leaf. This method works well because the glass extends close to ground level.

but this increases the heating cost exponentially. Open the ventilation in the greenhouse on days when the weather conditions allow.

Keep watering to a minimum, and if possible water in the mornings. The plants, even the defoliated dormant ones, should be kept with the root ball just moist, although they will normally stand being dry for a few days in the winter. For the plants in green leaf, quickly remove any dead or dying leaves to minimize the chances of botrytis. Turn the plants regularly and keep an eye out for any pests and diseases, treating if necessary.

In the later part of the winter season, encourage dormant plants to start into growth by spraying the hard wood, which will encourage buds to break. Plants in green leaf will start to grow as the day length increases, and you can take early cuttings from these plants. These cuttings are excellent for growing standards, or for any other forms of training needing a long growth period.

Standards and other trained shapes are best kept standing upright, either as dormant plants in the frost-free greenhouse, or ticking over in green leaf in the heated greenhouse. Being upright ensures that the sap rises to the head of a standard, and will initiate the new growths needed. For a pillar, cone or pyramid, it helps to suspend the plant horizontally, and rotate it in the horizontal axis, to ensure that all the lateral growths get some period of being vertical to boost the sap flow.

DORMANT PLANTS IN STORAGE

Check any plants in dormant storage periodically. Often books will tell you to keep the plants in an area just above freezing, with a temperature of

0–4°C (32–39°F). Realistically this is often difficult to achieve unless you have a cold cellar, or a garage kept frost-free in a cold climate. The essential part is to keep them above freezing and ensure they do not dry out.

If the temperature gets warmer for a period, dormant plants may start into growth, and when stored in the dark, produce long white straggly growths. Simply remove these. When it is warm enough to bring the plants out into the light they will start to make normal growth.

WARMER CLIMATES

If you are lucky enough to live in an area that is free from winter frosts, induce the dormancy period by pruning to reduce the size of the plant and promote new growth from the base.

Above Fuchsias grown from cuttings in late spring and not allowed to flower over the summer. These plants grow on in green leaf over the winter to make flourishing specimen plants the next year.

pruning a fuchsia

1 This 'Thalia' plant has been kept dormant through the winter, and is now starting to make new small growths.

2 Trim the wood of the branches back carefully just above the lowest strong buds, using sharp secateurs.

3 The aim is to obtain a fuchsia that is balanced in shape, with good growth from low down on the plant.

useful addresses

GENERAL

Eurofuchsia
http://www.eurofuchsia.org/
A European group founded in 1982 with membership and representation from a number of European national societies. There are links to many of the national European fuchsia societies. There is a European Registration system for new cultivars.

Fuchsia Research International
http://www.fuchsiaresint.org
An organization devoted to the history, preservation and discovery of the species fuchsias.

Find That Fuchsia
http://www.findthatfuchsia.info
Website by Rick Stevens; probably the largest list of fuchsias on the web, and some pictures.

Fuchsia Magic
http://www.fuchsiamagic.com/fuchsias/fuchsias.htm
Chris Martin's collection of fuchsia photographs.

Bonsai website
http://www.bonsaigarden.net/default.html
Kath van Hanegan's site with a lot about fuchsias and growing bonsai fuchsias.

'Dark Eyes'

Kenneth Nilsson's website
http://www2.dicom.se/fuchsias
An excellent site on fuchsias in Swedish and English with some interesting threads on fuchsia hardiness. This site originally hosted the Swedish Fuchsia Society's site.

Gelderse Fuchsia Info-Site
http://www.geldersefuchsia.info
A lot of useful information including Dutch winter hardiness tests and many fuchsia links, plus tips for searching for fuchsia websites; in Dutch/English.

Irene's website
http://home.hccnet.nl/boer.3/0
Interesting information and pictures; in Dutch/English.

Julio's Garden
http://fuchsiarama.com/index0.htm
Spanish/English language site.

Fuchsia Fairyland
http://www.fuchsia.tamsha.com.au/index.html
Australian site of Sue and Dave from Melbourne, with lovely pictures.

Jack Lamb's website
http://www.jacklamb.free-online.co.uk
UK national collection of species.

Dave Clark's website
http://www.fuchsiaclark.pwp.blueyonder.co.uk
Pictures of his raisings and a lot of useful information on fuchsia culture and hybridizing.

Barbara's fuchsia website
http://home.pacific.net.au/~bcooper1/fuchsia.htm
From the Blue Mountains near Sydney, Australia.

UNITED STATES

American Fuchsia Society
http://www.americanfuchsiasociety.org
The first national society, founded in 1929. It contains varied, interesting information and access to the AFS registration database for fuchsia cultivars online.

Northwest Fuchsia Society
http://www.nwfuchsiasociety.com
A lot of useful information and links.

SW Portland Fuchsia Club
http://swportlandfuchsia.org/index.html

Vallejo Branch of the American Fuchsia Society
http://westwood.fortunecity.com/rocco/83/fuchsia1.htm

Crescent City branch of the American Fuchsia Society
http://ccfuchsia.net
Interesting material about gall mite-resistant fuchsias.

Orange County branch of the National Fuchsia Society
http://dir.gardenweb.com/directory/ocbnfs
Basic contact information.

San Diego Fuchsia and Shade Plant Society
Secretary: Richard Hubbell,
15420 Olde Highway, 80#175,
El Cajon, CA 92021-2427
Tel: +1 619 443-3706

The Earthworks
http://www.fuchsias.net
18034 SE 248th St, Covington,
WA 98042

Weidners Nursery California
http://www.weidners.com/index.html
695 Normandy Rd, Encinitas,
CA 92024
Tel: +1 760 436-2194

Joy Creek Nursery
http://www.joycreek.com
20300 NW Watson Rd, Scappoose,
OR 97056
Tel: +1 503 543-7474
Fax: +1 503 543-6933

Monnier's Country Gardens LLC
http://www.monnierscountrygardens.com
17049 Mountain View LN NE Woodburn,
OR 97071
Tel: +1 503 981-3384

Roger's Gardens
http://rogersgardens.com/Fuchsias.asp
2301 San Joaquin Hills Rd,
Corona del Mar, CA 92625
Tel: +1 949 640-5800

'String of Pearls'

CANADA

British Columbia Fuchsia and Begonia Society
http://www.bcfuchsiasociety.com

Hong's Nursery
http://www.hongs.ca/products/annuals.asp
10582 - 120th Street, Surrey, BC, V3V 4G2
Tel: +1 604 588-3734
E-mail: gardens@hongs.ca

Richbar Nursery Ltd
http://www.richbarnursery.com/AboutUs_The
Greenhouse.asp
3028 Red Bluff Road, Quesnel, BC, V2J 6C6
Tel: +1 250 747-2915

Jolly Farmer Products Inc.
http://www.jollyfarmer.com
56 Crabbe Road, Northampton,
New Brunswick, E7N 1R6
Tel: +1 800 695-8300

UNITED KINGDOM

British Fuchsia Society
http://www.thebfs.org.uk
History of the society and other information.

Irish Fuchsia and Pelargonium Society
Secretary: Wilfie Fisher, 54 Copeland Cresc,
Comber, Newtownards, Co. Down, BT23 5HY,
Northern Ireland
Tel: +44 (0)28 9187 2151
E-mail: wilfred.fisher@btinternet.com

Bournemouth and Poole Fuchsia Society
http://www.bpfs.org.uk
A lot of useful information.

Salford and Bolton Fuchsia Society
http://www.users.zetnet.co.uk/gfoster
index2.htm
A lot of useful information and links. Look at
the fabulous fuchsias part.

**Waltham Forest Fuchsia and
Pelargonium Society**
http://www.communigate.co.uk/london/
fuchsia
Excellent website with society news, articles,
photos etc.

Walton Nurseries
http://www.waltonnurseries.co.uk/index.htm
Cherry Lane
Lymm, Warrington
Cheshire, WA13 0SY
Tel: +44 (0)1925 759 026
E-mail: info@WaltonNurseries.co.uk

Little Brook Fuchsias
http://www.littlebrookfuchsias.co.uk/Index.asp
Ash Green Lane West, Ash Green,
Nr Aldershot, Hampshire, GU12 6HL
Tel: +44 (0)1252 329 731
E-mail: carol@littlebrookfuchsias.co.uk

The Duchy of Cornwall Nursery
http://www.duchyofcornwallnursery.co.uk/
default.htm
Cott Road, Lostwithiel, Cornwall, PL22 0HW
Tel: +44 (0)1208 872 668
E-mail: sales@duchyofcornwallnursery.co.uk

Gower Fuchsias
http://gower-fuchsias.co.uk
Penclawdd Road, Penclawdd,
Swansea, SA4 3RB, Wales
Tel: +44 (0)1792 851 669
E-mail: sales@gower-fuchsias.co.uk

AUSTRALIA

Australian Fuchsia Society
http://users.chariot.net.au/~jmsa/fuchsia.htm
Society based in Adelaide, with lots of
information about fuchsias in Australia. Look
for the swan made out of fuchsia flowers.

Brenlissa Fuchsia Nursery
www.nurseriesonline.com.au/brenlissa
47 Wicklow Drive, Invermay Park, VIC 3350
Tel: +61 (0)4 3839 3578
E-mail: brenlissa@optusnet.com.au

Fuchsia Fantasy
75 Lillico Road, Lillico, TAS 7310
Tel: +61 (0)3 6428 2884

'Laura'

Jarrahdale Basket Nursery
Lot 452, Jarrahdale Rd, Jarrahdale,
WA 6124
Tel: +61 (0)8 9525 5329
E-mail: fuchsiajbn@bigpond.com

Metamorphosis Fuchsia Gardens
http://metphosi.customer.netspace.net.au/
index.htm
44 Hastings Avenue, Hoppers Crossing,
VIC 3029
Tel: +61 (0)3 9748 5562
E-mail: metphosi@netspace.net.au

NEW ZEALAND

**The National Fuchsia Society
of New Zealand**
http://nfsnz.orcon.net.nz
Also hosts the web pages of local fuchsia
groups in New Zealand.

Fuchsia 2000 Club
http://www.geocities.com/fuchia2000nz

Amberelle Fuchsias
156 Pickering Rd, RD 1, Cambridge
Tel: +64 (0)7 827 4375

Maidstone Nursery
S.H.1. Otaki North
Tel: +64 (0)6 364 7013
E-mail: buzz@xtra.co.nz

SOUTH AFRICA

Western Cape Fuchsia Society
http://www.fuchsiasoc.co.za/index.htm
Information and photos.

index

'Haute Cuisine'

'Tennesse Waltz'

F. denticulata

hardiness and zones

Plant entries in the directory of this book have been given hardiness descriptions and zone numbers. Hardiness definitions are as follows:

Tender: A plant which needs heated greenhouse protection through the winter in the local area.

Half-hardy: A plant which cannot be grown outside during the colder months in the local area and needs greenhouse protection through the winter.

Borderline hardy: A plant which, when planted outside, will survive through milder winters in the local area, with additional protection.

Hardy: A plant which, when planted outside, will survive reliably through the winter in the local area.

The zone numbers relate to each plant's hardiness. The zonal system used, shown below, was developed by the Agricultural Research Service of the United States Department of Agriculture. According to this system, there are 11 zones in total, based on the average annual minimum temperature in a particular geographical zone.

When a range of zones is given for a plant, the smaller number indicates the northernmost zone in which a plant can survive the winter, and the higher number gives the most southerly area in which it will perform consistently before suffering from an adverse heat-stress reaction.

This is not a hard and fast system, but simply a rough indicator, as many factors other than temperature also play an important part where hardiness is concerned. These factors include altitude, wind exposure, proximity to water, soil type, the presence of snow or shade, night temperature, and the amount of water received by a plant. These kinds of factors can easily alter a plant's hardiness by as much as two zones.

KEY TO ZONES

This map shows the zones in the United States. The temperature ranges apply worldwide.

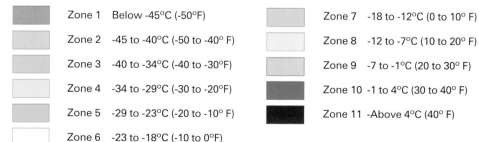

Zone 1 Below -45°C (-50°F)
Zone 2 -45 to -40°C (-50 to -40° F)
Zone 3 -40 to -34°C (-40 to -30°F)
Zone 4 -34 to -29°C (-30 to -20°F)
Zone 5 -29 to -23°C (-20 to -10° F)
Zone 6 -23 to -18°C (-10 to 0°F)
Zone 7 -18 to -12°C (0 to 10° F)
Zone 8 -12 to -7°C (10 to 20° F)
Zone 9 -7 to -1°C (20 to 30° F)
Zone 10 -1 to 4°C (30 to 40° F)
Zone 11 -Above 4°C (40° F)